THE SKIPPER
&
HER MATE

THE SKIPPER
&
HER MATE

Ten Years on Irish Waters

NICKI GRIFFIN

NEW ISLAND

The Skipper & Her Mate
First published 2013
by New Island
2 Brookside
Dundrum Road
Dublin 14

www.newisland.ie

PRINT ISBN: 978-1-84840-244-7
EPUB ISBN: 978-1-84840-245-4
MOBI ISBN: 978-1-84840-246-1

Typeset by JVR Creative India.
Cover design by Mariel Deegan.
Cover image by Nicki Griffin.
Printed by Bell & Bain Ltd, Glasgow.

10 9 8 7 6 5 4 3 2 1

Contents

Prologue   3

Chapter One   5

Chapter Two   25

Chapter Three   41

Chapter Four   57

Chapter Five   75

Chapter Six   91

Chapter Seven   109

Chapter Eight   129

Chapter Nine   153

Chapter Ten   169

Chapter Eleven   185

Chapter Twelve   201

Chapter Thirteen   217

Epilogue   231

Acknowledgments   233

Prologue

For thirteen years we had a five-year plan to move to Ireland. The desire began with a passion for traditional Irish music and was kept burning by trips in our camper van to Donegal, Clare and Galway. We walked the hills, I learned to drink Guinness and we went to every music session we could find. The plan began to fade, but then I was forced to give up my teaching job through ill health. My hiking and cycling days appeared to be over – expeditions outside the house were made in a wheelchair. The plan was resurrected.

In February 1996 we bought an acre with an old stone cottage in Co. Clare. There was a matching barn with half a roof, diverse mature trees and a mountain stream. We sold our house in Cheshire, Joe gave up his lecturing job and we moved to the West. In all my thirty-eight years I had never moved far from Cheshire, but Joe, Dublin-born, was returning to a country he had left at sixteen.

By 2000 we had completed a good deal of work on the house, and my health was improving, but not sufficiently for me to dig the garden or drive. I was struggling with feelings of being an outsider, of being English, of not belonging.

That was the year we discovered the Shannon and everything changed.

Chapter One

Shadows were sliding across the water as the lock gates opened and I started the boat engine. I was exhausted. We had left Portumna two hours before, travelling upstream in our hire boat towards Meelick, and now it was time to park. I had read about how to do this in the *Captain's Handbook* sent out to us weeks before. No doubt it was also part of the video presentation we had all been too nervous and excited to take in, but the ten minutes out-on-the-boat training had covered only reversing into a parking space. I had failed at that, and now feared doing the same with this sideways-on mooring.

The jetty was long and empty but for one boat. There was no current to worry about as we were on a stretch of canal, but I had no idea of how to proceed. The boat was pointed in the right direction, Joe beside me giving advice. Much too late we realised he ought to be outside, ready to do something useful with ropes.

A man appeared from the boat at the jetty giving an encouraging smile. By this stage Joe was on the patio at the back sorting out the tangle of line and panicking. I was wildly putting the boat into reverse then forward, reverse then forward. Boats don't have brakes, at least not in the conventional sense. 'Reverse' is the way you slow down or stop, and it takes some getting used to. Boats also move differently to road vehicles. If you turn a boat to the right, for example, the front goes right and the back goes left, which means you have to be aware of your rear end as well as your fore.

'Throw me the bow rope,' said the man on the jetty, then added helpfully, '... the one at the front.' The boat cracked off timber and Joe paused to glare at me as he made cautious progress up the side deck. He flung the rope at our adviser, who caught it deftly in one hand and tied it to a metal ring.

'Now I need the stern line.' The man gestured at me, and I gathered I was supposed to provide it. That sounded a better idea than trying to do anything more with the engine, so I scrambled outside and threw it.

Finally we were safely tied up with only one witness to our incompetence. I was shaking with anxiety and relief, but we'd had our first glimpse into a parallel river world quite different from anything experienced before. In Ireland we'd seen boats passing by when driving alongside Lough Derg, and in England I'd grown up next to a canal. My secondary school in Nantwich, a market town in South Cheshire, sat beside the Shropshire Union, where narrowboats were a part of everyday life. As with anything too familiar, though, I'd ignored them. I was beginning to see what I'd missed.

The *Captain's Handbook* showed Meelick to be a tiny place. Our mooring was not beside the village itself but at Victoria Lock, completed in 1844 and named after the then Queen of England (there is an Albert Lock further up the Navigation). The canal we'd entered via the lock was built to bypass the Keelogue Rapids – most of the Shannon rushes through the broad weir north of the lock. Above the weir a quay wall gives access to the village. Approaching the lock from the south you see a solid-looking stone building on a rise a little to the west. This is Meelick Church, founded as a Franciscan friary and in use since 1414 – a record among Catholic churches. It's the sweetest little church I've ever been inside, but is tricky to find if you approach by road: I played flute there for a colleague's wedding and half the party got lost on the way.

Before dinner we went for a stroll, and realised we were on an island between the canal and another bit of the Shannon. It's a confusing part of the river, splitting into many channels to form islands both north and south of the village. We walked across a wide timber bridge with dark, deep water beneath. This stretch of the Shannon, I discovered, had been widened in an attempt to alleviate flooding, for this is a very floody part of the country. In winter the fields are indistinguishable from the river – Meelick is in the Callows, the flood plain of the River Shannon. The Callows (from the Irish *caladh,* meaning river meadow) stretch for 50 km between Portumna and Athlone. Water meadows like this were commonplace in Europe before

extensive drainage, canal building and various hydro-
electric schemes changed them from wildlife haven to
year-round grazing land or riverside properties.

On the other side of the bridge we followed a
track across a boggy field and found another, smaller
stretch of water with an old, disused lock and lock
house (still lived in by the Victoria Lock-keeper). This
was the Cloonaheenogue Canal, the original Shannon
Navigation built in 1755 by Thomas Omer to avoid the
rapids at Meelick. There is still water below the lock,
but above it the channel has only a trickle and looks like
an oversized drain. Legs stretched, we went back to the
boat to try out the cooking facilities.

At quarter to nine the following morning boats
began to pile up on our jetty, waiting for the first lock.
We felt put out at the intrusion. The first lot went
through at nine, while we watched from the deck
with a cup of tea. We were excited (and edgy) about
heading off into unknown upstream waters. I studied
the *Captain's Guide* obsessively, hoping its information
would painlessly install itself.

Breakfast over, we stood on the jetty considering
how to get the boat off it, when a big cruiser pulled in
behind from the same Emerald Star fleet as ourselves.
We hovered uncertainly, ready to catch the ropes –
river camaraderie had already taken hold – and were
impressed with the skills of the man high up on the fly
bridge.

'How long have you been away?' I asked as, once
secured, he hopped onto the jetty with his wife and
two children.

'Since Thursday.'

'But you've been on a boat before?'

He laughed and shook his head. I must have looked incredulous.

'Are you only just out?' he asked. We nodded. I felt miserable, sure there was no way I'd ever be as confident as he was.

'You'll soon get the hang of it,' he said. 'I hadn't a clue when we took the boat. The main thing to remember is you don't have to reverse into a parking spot. Everyone goes in front first.'

Our new friend helped us leave by pushing the bow off the jetty, and I put the boat forward with fresh courage as the weight of parking terror lifted (a little) from my shoulders. We followed the broad and dreamy Shannon through the flat lands north of Meelick. Swinging its black, peaty water around slow bends, the river brought us back on ourselves again and again. Cruising from Meelick to Shannonbridge, only a few miles by road, took hours as the red-banded chimney of the power station came close and receded, came close and receded. Distant boats floated through grasses, turning on water we could not see. Herons rose in front of us, dropping to the river bank ahead to stand silent and waiting, rising to flap away with measured wings at our next approach, repeating the process over and over. Peewits tilted and banked, circling in the broad blue sky, sun flashing in neon blinks off their white fronts. I dreamed of my childhood and the rich fields of Cheshire where flocks of peewits rose and settled between Friesian dairy cows.

The Shannon Callows is a Special Area of Conservation and its flora and fauna are protected – it's of international importance for its bird life. Every winter a population of whooper swans gathers there in great flocks where they honk and hoot incessantly, gossiping as they fly low over the water. Hearing them, you quickly understand why they're called whoopers, and why, in contrast, our overwintering swans are called mute.

Other listed birds include the wigeon, golden plover, peewit and black-tailed godwit. The wonderfully named godwit sounds a bumbling idiot of a creature, without common sense, a hopeless wanderer, but in reality it's an elegant wader with remarkably long, slender legs. We saw one up to its belly in water, probing with its elongated bill for molluscs and worms.

The globally endangered corncrake is a summer visitor. It has a strange, creaking call that in the days of crowded cottages must have provided the backdrop to many courting couples seeking privacy in country lanes at dusk. The corncrake is a skulker, hiding in fields, apt to suddenly rise underfoot, no doubt startling those same courting couples whose ardour had taken them from the lane to the soft grass of the meadow. I'm still waiting to hear one.

It was afternoon when we rounded the last big bend in the river. Before us was a many-arched stone bridge and a quay wall full of boats. As we came close we could see there were no spaces; in fact cruisers were already doubled up.

'Oh God,' I said. 'What do we do?'

'Look. There's two hire boats. We could tie onto those.'

'Oh dear. D'you think we should? I'm not sure…'
I have always been a wimp about taking actions that might annoy other people. Joe has no patience with this type of nonsense, so we came alongside the designated boat, a twin of our own, circled with its necklace of fat green fenders. Two people came out smiling to take our ropes and I relaxed a small bit.

There is an etiquette involved in coming alongside another boat and tying up. The rules are largely unwritten and have to be learned through observation and experience, but we didn't yet know this. However, in spite of our ignorance the berthing went surprisingly well and nobody shouted at us. Soon we were settled and climbed gingerly across two boats to the shore, gripping every available handrail.

Shannonbridge is a single-street village with a couple of pubs, a shop and post office and one or two eateries. Its Napoleonic history had bequeathed an old stone fort, three batteries and a powder magazine. We had a Guinness in Killeen's at the top of the street and wandered back to the boat to think about dinner. Tied alongside us was a private boat. That made four boats in our raft; the row behind had five.

The river at Shannonbridge flows fast, and none of us novice skippers knew to put a line to the land. Each boat was tied only to the next, including the private boat, which should have known better. If the inner boat had come adrift in the night we would all have disappeared downstream, but ignorance allowed us to return with tranquillity to Killeen's to drink and talk and gawp. Every surface of the wall was covered with notices advising of upcoming events or warning against unwise behaviour. Foreign currency was pinned to the ceiling and people were mashed into every corner.

There was a shop attached to the pub into which the bar clientele drifted. Four German fishermen lined up behind the counter with fishing rods, hefting them and checking their worth. Hanging from beams were racks of pipes with variations of stem and bowl, sieves, hot-water bottles (with or without covers), pocket knives, bottle openers, tea strainers, fly swats and a card saying 'maggots and worms available'. On the shelves were Batchelor's soup, bottles of bleach, fishing flies, faded books about the Shannon, men's and women's habits (for burial) and loaves of bread.

We got talking to Nigel and Donna, a honeymoon couple from England hiring a Carrick Craft boat for a week. They'd started out from Banagher, the little town just upstream from Meelick.

'We'd planned to stay in Athlone tonight,' said Nigel. 'But we came up here for a drink and they kept giving us things.'

'Things?'

'Daft games. Then we'd go to leave and they'd come out with a photo album. And then a puzzle. So we had another hot chocolate and rum. Then another.'

Hot chocolate and rum was a Killeen's speciality. So was snuff. I had snuff down as something aristocrats from the nineteenth century used, but you could buy it in Killeen's, feed it into a contraption called a snuff catapult and shoot a pinch up each nostril, sending your sinuses into shock.

It was late when we arrived back at the quay. Some boats still had lights on, others had open curtains. The 'wall boat' in our raft was closed up and quiet, so we tiptoed across its deck. On the private boat next door, six people sat round a table in the saloon. Candles floated in a bowl of water amid plates and glasses and half-empty bottles of wine. Caught up in their conversation, they were oblivious to us, outsiders looking in.

We woke to commotion. I squinted at my watch. 8 a.m. Too early for noise. My head throbbed and I craved more sleep, but our boat was moving so we dragged on last night's clothes and went outside. The wall boat was ready to go. It had wanted to go since 6.30 a.m. and was not prepared to wait any longer. Its crew were untying ropes. A man appeared on the private boat.

'What are you doing? We never get up before twelve on the river!'

The poor wall boat people were visitors, a German couple wanting to make the most of their holiday instead of lying in bed. Arriving first on the previous day, they were snug against the quay before anyone else pulled in. Their morning was disappearing while the late-nighters snored in their bunks. Eventually, amid much grumbling, they slid away and the remaining raft was reattached to the wall.

It was tempting to go back to bed, but the river beckoned, and after rasher sandwiches we set off. I steered the boat through the winding waterway. More flat lands. More reed-lined flood plains. Turning a broad bend we could see old stone buildings on the eastern bank. Our chart told us this was the ancient settlement of Clonmacnoise. There were floating jetties that looked easy to get into, so we decided to stop for lunch. I went in nose first.

This used to be an important crossroads. When travelling north to south the Shannon was the main route, but east to west travellers used the Great Highway (known in Irish as the *Slí Mhór*). This road split the country in half from Dublin in the east to Clarinbridge, Co. Galway in the west. For the most part the Great Highway followed the Esker Riada, one of many eskers in Ireland. Eskers are gravel ridges, or more accurately a series of linear gravel hills that were formed after the glaciers of the last ice age retreated. In the early medieval period the Esker Riada was a major route for pilgrims and students travelling between the prominent religious settlements of Durrow and Clonmacnoise, or to and from the ports on the east and west of the country. It would have been used, too, by traders travelling from one fair to another, and by those going to the fairs.

The best time to be at Clonmacnoise is when all the coaches and their waterproofed passengers have returned to their hotels, and day-trippers have taken their picnics and children home. Then you can stand on the shores of the Shannon, close your eyes and imagine those distant people on their travels, stopping here for shelter and sustenance before continuing on their journeys. They would have heard the same sounds as you – the rustling of reeds as the wind riffles through, the bubbling trill of the dabchick. They would have seen a river that has barely changed, but the imaginative experience of the landscape as it stretched into the misty distance must have been quite different for those foot-weary travellers.

Leaving the jetty at Clonmacnoise was surprisingly easy. We'd gone in against the current, which is what you are supposed to do, although we didn't know it at the time, so once the boat's ropes were freed from the cleats it drifted backwards. Clear of the jetties, we turned and headed upstream towards Athlone.

As we neared the city a couple of hours later, we saw a boat parked in a field. It was on its side and didn't look comfortable. This stranding of boats, we learned, is a regular winter occurrence in the Callows, when the river disappears into its own flood. Just after the stranded boat was Athlone Lock. We were amazed by this lock – it was even bigger than the one at Meelick. The lock-keeper packed us in with a dozen other boats, the big gates creaked closed behind us, and we rose majestically to the next level to find ourselves in the centre of town.

Although we had no plans to stop in Athlone, we did wonder whether the boat needed fuel. We had no idea how far we could go on a tankful of diesel (as on most cruisers, there was no fuel gauge) and we were heading for Lough Ree, a big and rock-strewn lake. Beyond the quay walls and the public marina Joe spotted a fuel pump tucked away on the jetty of Athlone Cruisers, another hire-boat company.

'Go in there,' he said. I turned slowly and carefully to find the boat drifting to the right with the current.

'Give it more power!' I revved the engine and turned the wheel and we jolted to the left.

'Go on!' I came close to the jetty, then the current carried me away from it.

'Give it more power! Go back! It's shallow in there! Go left! Go forward! Go back! You're going aground!'

'You can damn well do it!' I abandoned the controls. Joe grabbed the wheel. The engine roared. We banged against the jetty. The current pulled us to the right. Another bang on the jetty.

'Don't need diesel anyway,' muttered Joe. He reversed into the main channel and turned upstream. There was silence as we passed the Lough Ree Yacht Club and cruised into the big, scary lake. We crept into a bottom corner where there was a public harbour attached to the Hodson Bay Hotel. Joe gave the controls back to me for parking. Nothing was said.

It was a relief to see the English honeymooners in the bar that evening – nothing like a third party to ease post-spat tension. We swapped notes and talked about going to the 'inner lakes' the next day. Apparently these lakes were small, beautiful and, because of their size and position, sheltered. Nothing like the rest of Lough Ree.

★★★

There was a choking sound, and the boat's engine cut out. We were halfway up the lake and I was at the wheel again. This had been the agreement. 'I don't mind going,' Joe had said earlier that summer when I brought up the subject of a boat on the Shannon. 'But you'll have to drive.'

'OK.' I liked this idea. I hadn't been able to drive a car for any distance for the last few years due to a chronic pain condition – but I thought I might manage a boat with only hand controls.

I turned the key, but nothing happened.

'Leave it!' said Joe. 'You might do some damage.'

We were outside a little bay called Blackbrink, and there were no other boats in sight. The lake was calm and the water silky. Joe went to the bow and pushed the anchor overboard. It took hold, which was lucky as we had no idea how this should be done. It isn't just a matter of lowering the hook to the lakebed – an anchor won't hold on rock or loose mud or a weedy bottom. You need to approach your anchoring spot upwind or against the current or tide if there is one. At the chosen place, stop the boat, drop the anchor overboard then feed out between five and seven times the length of chain it takes to hit the bottom (more chain for heavier weather). Reverse slowly until the anchor catches, then observe your surroundings to make sure it isn't dragging.

'We'll have to phone Emerald Star,' I said. Part of the boat's equipment was a mobile phone dedicated to this purpose. Emerald Star said they would send out an engineer. We waited, read our books, looked at the view and hoped the wind didn't rise. An hour later the phone rang.

'I can see you but I can't get to you,' said the engineer, who had no boat. 'I'm trying to find one of the fleet to bring me out.'

Eventually a big Emerald Star cruiser appeared, heading straight towards us. It had the engineer on board. The boat came alongside and he hopped onto our side deck.

'Have you been in the canal?' he said.

'No no,' we replied, but this was a lie. The start of the canal was in Blackbrink Bay and it led to a village called Lecarrow. The relevant page in the *Captain's Handbook* had a Navigation notice which said, 'Beware of reeds. Possibility of engine damage'. The canal was, indeed, full of floating green vegetation. 'Just a little way,' said Joe, 'to see'. We ventured cautiously into the narrow waterway, but lost our nerve part way down and turned back. Now we were afraid of engine damage and blame.

The engineer took up the floor and fiddled around.

'There's your problem. Weed in the trap.'

On a boat, water is sucked from the lake (along with weeds and other floating matter) to keep the engine cool. To prevent damage, the water first passes through a trap designed to catch weeds and debris. Too much stuff in the trap and the water can no longer pass through to do its job.

'They've been cutting weed in the canal,' said the engineer as he stood up and started the engine. He gave us a big smile. 'I'd say that was your problem. Can you drop me at Portrunny? It's just up the lake a bit.'

★★★

A curious thing happens to perspective when you're on a large body of water. The physical Lough Ree looks utterly different to the lake on the chart. Islands that on paper appear to be on the left float hazily on the distant right, and the markers that show the way (black for starboard and red for port) swap places, so confusing unwary travellers. It was late afternoon and we were headed for the inner lakes, but were confused about distance and direction. The chart was full of Navigation notices warning of rocks and shoals: Wood Shoal, Cornamissoge Rocks, Adelaide Rock, and, worst of all, Hexagon Shoal, which carries its own Navigation warning – 'most dangerous rock on the Shannon'.

To get to the inner lakes, you had to pass what looked on the chart to be close to this terror. To avoid this, we went the long way round, travelling from one marker to the next instead of across the lake. Our boat moved very slowly. We were tired and relieved when eventually we arrived at the entrance to Killinure Lough, the first of the inner lakes.

'So where now?' I asked the navigator, who turned the *Captain's Handbook* sideways and frowned. I gazed at the lake and relaxed – it was edged by tall reeds and millpond still. A handful of coots scuttled away as we idled along. All we needed was to find a place to tie up for the night. We passed a marina on the left, but it was private and of no use to those in rented boats. Joe checked the chart again, looking for the public jetties. Water stretched away to the left, and we approached two other marinas full of boats, but each had the same notice: 'Private. Berth holders only'.

I stopped the boat in the middle of the final lake, despondent. There were no public harbours or jetties or any likely spot at all. I stared ahead and Joe peered at the chart. I had no desire to return to Hodson Bay. We were on an adventure, a voyage of exploration, and I wanted to stay *here* in these gorgeous lakes.

'Go a bit further,' said Joe.

'What's the point?'

'There's boats ahead.' In the distance was a line of cruisers.

'Another private marina. No point.'

I did as he asked anyway, and drawing close we could see the boats were attached to a jetty. Some of them had green liveries identical to our own. We crept around to the far side, and I steered slowly into a gap halfway along. Joe jumped off with one rope, I with another, and we tied the boat to the cleats on the timber planking with surprisingly little shouting. As we stepped back on board feeling pleased with ourselves, a well-pressed fellow in shirt and tie appeared on the jetty. My mood plummeted. We were going to be told to move.

'Do you have a reservation?' he said.

'No.'

'Would you like one?' We were silent for a moment before we caught on. A glance to the right showed a sign we had missed. There was a restaurant on the shore and we were in the boat park. Unless we wished to eat here, we would not be able to stay. The decision was instant and unanimous.

'Yes please.'

Having booked a table for 8 p.m., we walked ashore to have a look at the place. The building was long and glass-fronted with a verandah, and inside we glimpsed linen-covered tables set with solid-looking cutlery and tall wine glasses. The restaurant was called the Wineport and the menu suggested class.

We returned to our boat to have showers and see if we could muster a decent set of clothes each. Feeling smug, we walked the few yards to claim our table overlooking the lake. Just inside the door we saw the honeymooners nibbling at their starters. We exchanged knowing smiles. The setting was fabulous, and it was a restaurant that seemed to have everything. There were even Tampax in bowls in the Ladies. We savoured three slow courses and some excellent wine, then sat beside the fire and drank more brandy than was good for us.

I woke with a start. There was something banging. The boat gave a shudder then rocked. Jesus. I looked to see was Joe awake.

'What was that?' I squawked. He was awake.

'Don't know!' *Bang. Bang.* I sat up and peered out of the window. I could see enough to know there were white-topped waves on this lake we'd imagined to be always calm, and could feel enough to know that we were hopelessly exposed to a rising wind. The hire boat had come with its own dinghy attached, and it was this that was slamming against the hull. As the night wore on and sleep deprivation took its toll, outrage at the banging supplanted a fear of drowning. Just before dawn I went outside in my nightdress and pulled the dinghy close, tying it as tight as I could. The banging was replaced by a vile squeaking, and it was only when the wind died as brightness crept through the curtains that I finally slept.

The following morning we adjusted our ropes, pulling the boat in as tight as we could and winding several figures of eight around the cleat until the mess resembled a ball of wool. We found our honeymoon friends had done the same. These 'balls of knitting' can be seen attached to hire boats up and down the Shannon, and we persisted with the practice for the rest of the week. It is entirely unnecessary. A 'round turn' in which you pass the rope end around the cleat or bollard, then around again, will hold much of the boat's weight. A figure of eight, and possibly one 'locking turn', will do the rest. Also, squashed fenders on a boat that is drawn in hard against the quay will squeak all night as they rub up and down. Far more comfortable to give the boat space to drift a few inches in and out.

We were halfway through the week, and it was time to start our journey back to Portumna. This was when we began the game called 'What if We Had a Boat Ourselves'. Smitten with this hidden riverworld, we had no wish to give it up. The previous couple of years had not been easy – we'd been doing up a place that was practically derelict while living in it – and the Shannon was a release for both of us. Even by the second day of our holiday we'd begun to relax into each other's company in a way we hadn't done for far too long.

Between Banagher and Meelick on our way upstream we'd noticed a side channel off to the left.

The tops of boats suggested a harbour or marina, and the chart marked it as Shannon Grove. Coming downstream Joe persuaded me it would be a good idea to go and have a look. There were vessels of all types tied to a labyrinth of jetties. I was nervous as we pulled in: there were people watching. But my driving skills had improved since that first day, and we managed to not disgrace ourselves. After we'd secured the boat, we realised that the jetty had no access to land, so Joe took the dinghy and zig-zagged across to the little marina. Half an hour later he returned, erupting with enthusiasm.

'I've found a wonderful boat! This old fellow brought me inside and showed me all the storage. Lots of wood. It's called a Freeman 22. He said it would be the perfect starter boat for us.'

'We're only playing at this,' I said.

'Yes yes, of course. It's just a game.'

We called at Shannon Harbour, the point where the Grand Canal joins the river, and were thrilled at the number of boats for sale. We took optimistic photographs of wrecks, and told each other how much cheaper they were than we'd expected.

★★★

The hire-boat trip had taken only the first week, of our fortnight's holiday. Each day of the second week we loaded our dogs Aoife and Frankie (retrieved from their stay with friends) into the car, and explored every tiny boatyard and harbour around nearby Lough Derg.

Joe asked endless questions of anyone he could find. He's very good at that, and one thing you will never be short of on the waterways is advice; whether or not it is good you have to decide for yourself. This in-depth research led us to one conclusion: the old man in Shannon Grove had been right.

We spent the money we'd saved for a deep-bore well on a boat. Liam Flanagan, who owned the well-drilling rig, couldn't do anything for another few months, so we decided that water for the house would have to wait. We wanted to float on it instead.

There were two Freeman 23s for sale in Ballina at the south end of Lough Derg. The Freeman 23 was one foot longer than the 22: we would come to realise that in a boat of that size a foot makes quite a difference, but at the time we were ignorant of such subtleties. The first boat we looked at, the cheaper of the two, was in poor condition inside and the engine was dodgy. The second, however, was far more promising. The best thing of all was that the owner was returning to England in something of a hurry, catching a ferry the following week and eager to sell before he went. We could afford to buy it outright. On 20 September 2000 we became the very proud and slightly bemused owners of *Towed In A Hole*.

Chapter Two

*O*nce upon a time, all boats were made of timber, steel or possibly iron, but by the 1950s this ancient tradition of boat making was under threat from a new and very modern substance: fibreglass. Made from filaments of glass, it was developed in the 1930s as an insulating material – for which it is still used today. It has other names: glass fibre; fibre-reinforced polymer (FRP); glass-reinforced plastic (GRP). people believed that boats made from this stuff would last for decades.

Joe and I learned that Freeman Ltd, the manufacturer of our new boat, had an excellent reputation for robust, well-put-together cabin cruisers. *Towed In A Hole* was made from heavy fibreglass, thicker than that found in modern vessels. We were told this was because she was constructed before the 1973-4 oil crisis, when the price of crude (used in making GRP) went through the roof. This seems plausible, but economics is not my subject and it could well be apocryphal. However, it made us feel that we had a very solid boat that was less likely to be punctured on the submerged rocks we were terrified of hitting.

Before the Second World War, John Freeman made caravans in Stoke Golding, a small village on the Leicestershire border, but in 1957 he turned his skills to the nautical. He moved to Wolvey, just over the border in Warwickshire, where by the 1970s he was employing 125 workers and turning out four or five cruisers a week. The Freeman boats were of a style that, like many on the Norfolk Broads, appealed to non-boating people – water caravaners in other words – but possibly appalled the real sailors of the time. Instead of bunks and sea-going qualities, the Freeman vessels had a comfortable, caravan-style interior. *Towed In A Hole* may have been plastic on the outside, but she had beautiful cabinet-making craftsmanship inside: the veneer on cupboards and fittings for each boat were made from one tree to ensure a match of grain and colour. Boat hire companies on the Shannon bought fleets of them, the different lengths (22 ft to 41 ft) being suitable for every size of family – this was how our cruiser had started its life in Ireland.

Freeman cruisers still have a large and loyal following. When John Freeman retired, the company stopped making new boats, but all the parts are still available from John Freeman (Sales) Ltd based on the River Thames in Moulsford, Oxfordshire. From the Freeman website you can purchase burgees (small flags to tie to your mast), fleeces and the *Owners' Handbook*. There's a Freeman Owners Club, which organises Fun Days and other social events, along with providing an information service, a shop and a newsletter. There's also a Freeman Cruiser Fan Club (not to be confused with the Owners Club), upon whose website home page a Freeman boat apparently levitates. Here you can discuss all things Freeman and post a photograph of your boat beside her vital statistics.

When we bought *Towed In A Hole* she was berthed in a marina at the very south of Lough Derg, a body of water that sprawls through submerged valleys for 32 km from Portumna in the north to the twin towns of Killaloe and Ballina in the south. Here the river narrows through mountains for its final descent to the sea. The towns are separated by a handsome thirteen-arch road bridge, originally constructed around 1770, but rebuilt and extended over the following centuries. The bridge has well-designed pedestrian refuges, which is just as well – it's very narrow, and until recently took two-way traffic. Now there are six-way traffic lights and at least one frustrated driver (Joe) on their way to work in Limerick.

We had a few days' grace before we needed to move *Towed In A Hole* from her old berth. Joe managed to secure temporary lodgings in a tiny harbour that was part of a holiday complex not too far from Killaloe in Tinerana Bay. At home, we feverishly studied our *Captain's Guide,* and were distressed to learn that in order to reach this safe haven we had to cross a hatched area, marked on the chart as out of bounds to hire boats because it was dangerous and shallow and possibly contained dragons. However, we took advice and learned that if we took a straight course across

Tinerana Bay we would avoid all shoals and other dangers.

Venturing onto Lough Derg for the first time in *our own boat* was both thrilling and alarming. North of Killaloe for perhaps half a mile the river was enclosed by friendly banks with houses, trees and other familiar, land-based objects. Then we passed through two markers for left and right, and found ourselves in the open lake, where anything could happen. Water stretched north in a misty expanse. The banks were no longer within swimming distance. Joe was in charge of directions, and we kept going until he judged it was time to turn and take our straight course in. This sounded simple, but the harbour entrance was not easy to spot and there were no markers to guide us. Joe positioned himself at the front as lookout, anxiously peering into the water, and I drove cautiously forward. The narrow opening, bordered by tightly mown grass and well-manicured bushes, came into view. We puttered through the small cut, and there was the little harbour we'd visited by land. At the end of it was our berth.

The next ordeal was to tuck *Towed In A Hole* into her designated place. Turning a boat with a single engine in a small space is not as simple as, well, just turning. Because the boat pivots, you have to do a forwards and backwards manoeuvre, steadily easing the length of the boat into the required position. I turned towards the gap between timber jetties without a problem, but she wasn't anywhere near straight. Into reverse, then forward, then reverse. I could feel Joe fidgeting beside me – as though he could do any better. Eventually, I had the nose close to the timber boards, and Joe hopped off. We pulled her in the rest of the way with ropes. Could do better....

From this safe haven we went a little further every day, tentative as a small child edging towards independence. Like the child, though, we needed to know that security was close by. We pottered about the south of the lake, content with small adventures. One afternoon, we decided it would be a splendid thing to explore Tinerana Bay. We had overcome our fear of dragons, so ventured into hatched corners.

'Let's try in there,' said Joe, who is more intrepid (or foolhardy) than I.

'I don't think we should.'

'You never want to do things I suggest.'

A short while later we were balanced on what we took to be a rock. My husband has a tendency to assume the worst in such situations, so for the first few minutes we panicked, expecting the boat to sink.

'We'll have to phone Angus,' said Joe. 'He'll come and rescue us.' We had recently bought a mobile phone, so could do this. Angus Leavie was the first owner of *Towed In A Hole* when she was part of the now-modernised hire boat fleet he ran from Williamstown, halfway up the lake.

Williamstown used to have a hotel, and was a main station for the Inland Steam Company when boats used to carry passengers and freight up and down the Shannon. There's a connection between Williamstown and Killaloe, which I first came across by way of a ballad

I heard sung at a traditional music session in Feakle in
Co. Clare. The song tells of how, in November of 1920,
a time of martial law in Clare, three men who were on
the run and hiding at Williamstown were captured. The
Black and Tans, ex-servicemen paid ten shillings a day
by the British Government to suppress rebellion, had
commandeered the steamer *Shannon* in Killaloe to take
them to Williamstown. They discovered the fugitives at
Williamstown House and brought them, along with the
caretaker of the house, back to Killaloe. At around midnight the four men were taken onto the bridge and shot.
They became known as the Scariff Martyrs, and there
is a plaque to their memory at the centre of the bridge.

Angus Leavie was well used to agitated beginners in boats. He also had intimate knowledge of the
topography of the lake.

'Where are you?' Joe described our location.

'Is there any water coming in?' A flurried look
around.

'Can't see any.'

'You're probably on a sandbank. Try rocking her
and pushing off with the boat-hook. You do have a
boat-hook?'

'I think so.' We did. We calmed ourselves and
pushed and rocked and suddenly we were afloat. A
sheepish phone call told Angus the good news.

Shortly after this incident, we went all the way to
Mountshannon on the northern shore of Scariff Bay.
Joe had discovered an organisation called the Inland
Waterways Association of Ireland (IWAI), which we
joined, needing all the help we could get, and the local

branch was having an end-of-season weekend. The people on the boat next to us in the harbour were very friendly. Fergal, the owner, invited us aboard and introduced Jim, his crew for the weekend.

'Do you have three-foot-longer syndrome yet?' asked Jim.

'What's that?'

'Everyone always wants a boat that's three foot longer.'

'But we've only just bought this one,' we protested.

'You'll see.'

★★★

We tried to get used to the name, to think of it with amusement and even affection, but it was impossible. We were unable to keep our heads up on the river in a boat called *Towed In A Hole*. Carl, the previous owner, was an enthusiastic fan of Laurel and Hardy, the comedy duo who made films together in the first half of the twentieth century. He named his boat after the vessel in the 1932 film of the same name. Maybe if we'd been fans too ....

When we bought the little Freeman our acquaintance with boat lore was limited, but one thing we did know was that renaming a boat was certain to lead to misfortune. What were we to do? The choice was less difficult than expected: we feared humiliation more than disaster.

If you tell people you are going to rename your boat they will often look at you askance, resisting at first the temptation to tell you 'No! Don't do it!' but quickly succumbing. 'Don't you know it's bad luck?' they say, looking abashed, or making a joke, for this is the twenty-first century and one shouldn't believe such things.

There are many stories of the woe that comes from giving your boat a different name. A warning to us all is found in Robert Louis Stevenson's *Treasure Island*. Silver is holding forth:

> He was hanged like a dog, and sun-dried like the rest, at Corso Castle. That was Roberts' men, that was, and comed of changing names to their ships – Royal Fortune, and so on. Now what a ship was christened, so let her stay, I say.

And so might Ernest Shackleton have said when his ship *Endurance* became trapped in sea ice at the beginning of his 1914 voyage to the Antarctic. *Endurance* was held fast in frozen waters for ten months. The ship was steadily crushed by the ever-moving ice until the crew had to abandon it. Shackleton and his crew survived. The ship did not. *Endurance* had been renamed – when launched she was christened *Polaris*.

The origins of the renaming superstition are believed to lie in the classical myth of Poseidon, Greek god of the sea, who, it is said, keeps a record of every boat in the water. He is displeased at any attempt to change this record and so brings disaster on the offending vessel. Martine Cuypers, a Classics scholar at Trinity College, Dublin, says she's never encountered this piece of lore in an ancient text. At best, she says, 'it derives from some report about ritual/custom in a relatively late author (say, Plutarch) but more likely has been cooked up far more recently.' I enjoyed Martine's reference to Plutarch as a relatively late author: he was born in AD 46.

The allusion to ritual and custom sounds plausible. While looking for something else on my bookshelves I came upon *The Myths and Legends of Ancient Greece and Rome*, with the subtitle *Being a popular account of Greek and Roman Mythology*. Written by EM Berens, this sixth edition was published in 1892 and, while there is no mention of the superstition, it does have this to say about Poseidon:

> He possessed the power of causing at will, mighty and destructive tempests ... On the other hand, his alone was the power of still-ing the angry waves, of soothing the troubled waters, and granting safe voyages to mariners.

In fishing communities Poseidon was both feared and revered, and was invoked and propitiated by a liba-tion before a voyage and profuse thanks afterwards. Keeping to customs and rituals would be an important part of averting Poseidon's displeasure, so unneces-sary changes would doubtless be avoided, particularly among those who regularly trespassed upon the ter-ritories of such an unpredictable god. And how would Poseidon know which boats to treat kindly if people were in the habit of giving them new names?

Not everybody believes that changing a boat's name will necessarily bring *bad* luck. Colin Becker, a long-time boater on the inland waterways, says:

> The story I always heard was that changing the name of a boat would change the 'luck' of the boat. So it was unwise to change the name of a 'lucky' boat and a good idea to change the name of an 'unlucky' one.

After hearing this, I thought again about our Freeman 23 and realised happily that the 'Becker Rule' applied. When we first saw *Towed In A Hole,* she had a broken window. The damage had been done by the foot of Carl's angry and recently estranged wife. They had bought *Towed In A Hole* together from Angus Leavie's boat-hire company, but grave misfortune had clearly overcome their relationship: Carl left Ireland alone to return to his native England.

Some boating superstitions have a practical purpose. For example, sailors have long had the idea that whistling on board will call up a wind, and some yachtsmen still try this when becalmed: 'whistling for a wind' in everyday parlance has come to mean wishing for the impossible. Yet whistling on board ship has frequently been forbidden. This is sensible – on a ship, orders are piped by the boatswain or bosun and a sailor whistling is likely to cause confusion – but a superstition has taken hold that whistling on a ship at sea will induce a storm in which all will perish.

Francis Bacon suggested in 1605 that superstitions often begin with a specific event, particularly where success or disaster has occurred:

> The mind of man, if a thing have once been existent, and held good, receives a deeper impression thereof, than if the same thing far more often failed and fell out otherwise: which is the root, as it were, of all superstition and vain credulity.

Other superstitions are based on prejudice. It is supposedly unlucky to have a woman on board as she will cause the seas to rise up and engulf the ship, or she will lead the poor men, weak-willed creatures, into vice.

These stories go back centuries. The main works of English chronicler Raphael Holinshed were published in 1577, and his writings were used by Shakespeare as the source of many history plays, but they also document maritime expeditions. Sir John Arundel was sent by Henry IV, the King of England, to give aid to the Duke of Brittany. His fleet set out in 1379 from Southampton, but got into difficulties when hit by a storm. The ships were scattered, and Arundel's vessel was driven onto the coast of Ireland, where it foundered. Robert Southey, Romantic poet, biographer, historian and all-round scholar, reported in *The Early Naval History of England* (1835) that twenty-five ships were lost, with many horses and 1,000 men. Arundel was among the dead. According to Southey, Holinshed believed these men deserved their fate. He said that:

... outrageous wickedness was justly punished, and that the catastrophe which befell these men was regarded as a judgment; for not content with abusing men's wives and daughters in the ports before they took ships, they carried them off with them to sea – by persuasion or by force – and when the tempest raged they threw them overboard ...

More than sixty women perished, tipped into the water by sailors desperate to calm the wild ocean. Holinshed suggests 'that they thought so long as they had such women aboard with them, whom they had abused so long, God would not cease the rage of the tempest.'

There's no record in my ship's log of when *Towed In A Hole* officially changed her name, but a trawl through our photographic archive gives some clues. Early pictures show her as *Towed In A Hole* with the original navy blue canopy covering the cockpit. Photographs taken the following spring, in which she sports a fine new wine-coloured canopy, display the new name. The missing link is provided by a photo of the boat in Rossmore, a secluded harbour near the top of Lough Derg. In this she has the blue canopy, but no name at all. We must have peeled off the old vinyl *Towed In A Hole* sticker and gone naked.

Brazen though we were about abandoning the name *Towed in a Hole*, we were not completely unaffected by superstition. We thought it prudent to appease the lake's own Poseidon and protect ourselves from underwater ogres. We decided to hold a ceremony, but first we would have to choose a new name, a task that took most of the winter. In the meantime, in preparation, I sewed up a little pouch with propitious herbs inside and embroidered runic symbols of protection on the front.

This task gave me something to do when we were stranded in the small lakeside settlement of Garrykennedy on the Tipperary shore of the lake. There were two harbours in those days: the old public harbour with its high stone walls, metal-runged ladders and steps built for (or by) giants, and the council harbour full of local sailing and fishing boats.

Perched on the edge of the old harbour is a broken-down castle built by the O'Kennedys in 1480 to control what must have been a significant port on the Shannon. A stone quay leads into this harbour, probably constructed in the late 1700s. The harbour itself was built in 1829 by the Steam Navigation Company, purportedly using stone from the old castle. There's a tune called 'Garrykennedy Castle' written by Paddy O'Brien, a musician of some renown from Newtown, near Nenagh in Co. Tipperary. It's a hornpipe and a fine tune, as are all his compositions, many of which are named after local places: 'Newtown Bridge', 'The Arra Mountains', 'The Old Road to Garry'.

There is also 'The Hangover', another hornpipe, which very likely refers to the consequences of playing tunes in the Barge Inn, the pub owned by Dan

Larkin in Garrykennedy, a favourite place for traditional music sessions that would often go on until dawn. Dan Larkin was a fiddle player and, along with Paddy O'Brien, a member of the Ormond Céilí Band.

The Barge Inn is still tucked behind the harbour in Garrykennedy, but these days it's called Larkin's Bar. We had a drink there on the night of our stranding – what else could one do? We *had* attempted to leave, setting out into a lake that had nasty, choppy waves coming from the south west. We'd learned in our few weeks on the river that beam-on waves (those hitting you on the side) would make the boat rock, breaking crockery and causing alarm among people and canines, but we would be all right today, we reassured each other. Our route back to Tinerana Bay would allow us to head straight into the waves, and we'd been told that a Freeman 23 was very unlikely to sink, even though it may feel like riding a champagne cork in a flushed toilet. We cheered ourselves with the will-not-sink angle, and set off in good form, chugging slowly out of the harbour, but as soon as we came out of the lee and into the wind, the boat mutated into a cork.

'I'm not very happy,' said Joe.

'Neither am I.'

'And we have to go round Parker Point.' We both had strained, under-the-surface-panic voices. Parker Point is a notoriously dangerous section of Lough Derg where the southerly arm joins Scariff Bay. A strong south-westerly splits around the headland opposite the

Point, pushing waves from south and west to meet in pyramids at the intersection. Pyramids provide beam-on waves from every side.

In the winter of 1946, *45M*, a 60 ft Grand Canal Company boat, was working its way from Dublin to Limerick with a cargo of porter, and had reached Lough Derg. There was a strong wind, so they pulled into Garrykennedy to take shelter. The *St James*, a working tug, also drew into the harbour. By late afternoon the skipper of *45M* made the decision to continue and set off towards Killaloe, the tug following shortly after. While en route the *St James* took *45M* under tow, a common occurrence in a time of fuel shortages.

As they reached Parker Point the wind strengthened to gale force. The waves must have been coming from every direction and they, or the high winds, caused the cargo on *45M* to shift. The barge listed and waves washed across her decks. The tow rope snapped. Within minutes, *45M* sank. Ned Bolan, Jimmy McGrath and Jack Boland went down with her. Tony Brien struggled to the shore. One can only imagine the horror and helplessness of the crew on the *St James* as they watched *45M* sink.

For twenty-nine years, *45M* lay on the bed in the deeps of Lough Derg, lost but not forgotten, until in 1975 she was salvaged and found to be in surprisingly good condition. In 1976 she was sold to David Coote, who restored both hull and Bolinder engine. In 1980 the boat was reintroduced to the waterways of her working days.

We didn't know this story when we set out from Garrykennedy that day, but our boat felt very small in this big, grey sea.

'We're here to enjoy ourselves, not be terrified,' said Joe firmly, words that were to become a mantra over the coming months. We turned back.

Chapter Three

That winter, *Towed In A Hole* was lifted from the water by Angus Leavie at the hire-boat company Shannon Castle Line, from whom, not so many years ago, families of four would rent this Freeman 23 for a week on the river. Boats made from GRP were normally taken out in winter and stored on blocks, allowing the hull to dry out and helping to control a boat sickness, commonly known as osmosis, in which the gelcoat (the outer layer) begins to blister. Over the years there has been earnest discussion about how much osmosis threatens the longevity of a boat, with some people claiming it isn't a problem at all: that it may be unsightly, but as it occurs on the hull this hardly matters. These are often the people trying to sell you a boat with osmosis. *Towed In A Hole* had blisters. We pierced one to see what would happen, and a little ooze of liquid appeared with a sharp, chemical smell. We were told this acidic 'blister juice' can break down the polyester in a boat's gelcoat and cause weakness in the GRP laminate. This made us anxious, even though we were assured that osmosis in a boat built in

1976 was normal. The illness, said our advisors, though chronic, could be controlled with relative ease.

We visited our boat every so often during that winter and marvelled that she belonged to us. Joe dealt with the osmotic blisters by scraping them out and pressing car body filler into the revealed hollow, definitely not the procedure advised by official 'osmosis treatment centres' providing 'full treatment' involving removal of the entire gelcoat, at great expense. However, do-it-yourself boating magazines suggested grinding out the blisters, letting them dry, and filling them with epoxy paste. Some specify *not* car body filler, but Joe was always one to make up his own mind.

In the spring of 2001, we washed the boat carefully, returned her to the water and cruised to the top of the lake to a new marina in Cloondavaun Bay, where we had taken a berth.

The time came for our self-designed renaming ceremony. I picked handfuls of petals from a pink, highly scented rambling rose-bush at home, and Joe put the bubbly in a cold bag filled with ice. We chose Mountshannon as the venue not only for its location, with views out to the holy island of Iniscealtra, but also (and mainly, it must be admitted) because it had floating pontoons, not common in 2001. These sat just above the water, low enough to allow for the application of the self-adhesive name to the bow.

The weather was fine as we puttered into the harbour and secured *Towed In A Hole* to the pontoon. Half an hour later we were ready, and I looked round carefully to see if anybody was looking. The place was empty, it being midweek, so I edged onto the narrow deck, clutching my bag of perfumed rose.

'OK?' I said to Joe. He nodded, and I set off round the perimeter, clinging to the handrail. The process was ungainly but well meant, and I sprinkled petals on the water until we were encircled with dusty pink, making supplications to the gods and goddesses, the fates and the future. The little bag of herbs so carefully sewn in Garrykennedy was tucked into a storage compartment in the fore cabin.

Having attended to the spiritual side of the ritual, we bent to the task of applying the name. All you had to do was peel off the backing and fix it on, preferably without wrinkles. We hauled in the bow, smoothed on the name, had a sharp discussion about whether it was straight, then turned the boat around to get at the other side. The job done, we stood back to admire our work. Joe popped the cork on the bottle of champagne and *Towed In A Hole* officially became *Caoimhe*.

People ask why we chose the name *Caoimhe* (pronounced 'kweeva' for those with no Irish), but I don't have a ready answer. We went through several dozen birds and mammals searching for something appropriate, but either they didn't seem right or someone else had got there first. So we thought an Irish name would do – that for a girl, not a boy (boats being female). *Caoimhe* means gentle and graceful, which we hoped our boat would be, and we found the sound of it pleasing.

Looking for Irish names, is easier in these less-religious (and internet-informed) days than it used to be. Many years ago Joe worked in an Irish wolfhound kennels in England. The owner liked to give her dogs Irish names and had run out of ideas for the next batch of puppies, so Joe wrote to his aunt in Dublin asking her to send him a book of baby names. He explained why he wanted it – probably to avoid her leaping to conclusions not suitable for a young and unmarried Catholic boy. He soon received a response – how could he think of naming a dog after a saint? On no account would she send him such a book. He should be ashamed of himself.

It was shortly after the renaming that we set off on our Big Adventure. So far the longest we'd stayed on the boat was a weekend, but this was to be an eight-day voyage. We planned to go up the Shannon, revisiting Athlone and the inner lakes, then cruising across Lough Ree to Lanesborough and beyond.

We left our berth at Cloondavaun on the last Sunday of May, and crossed the top of Lough Derg to enter the narrowing river at Portumna. The dogs were aboard, along with more supplies than we could possibly need, and we were full of excitement and trepidation. This time we would do things properly. We had three months' more experience than the last time we'd come this way, and I was looking forward to practising my driving skills.

We spent our first night in Shannon Harbour, where we'd first seen all those boats for sale – it gave us a thrill to return there on a *private* boat. Next day we set out again along the winding river to Athlone, an easy cruise with a lunch stop at Clonmacnoise, arriving in Athlone in late afternoon. I felt so much more confident this time as I brought *Caoimhe* into the lock, but then, quite suddenly, we were sideways. There was a stiff beam-on breeze, and our light, little boat decided she would be happier pointing straight at it.

Sideways in a lock is always humiliating. The lock-keepers are wonderful and have seen it all before, but you cannot help thinking they're silently mocking your incompetence. Passers-by enjoy the spectacle, and other boat owners smirk at each other while standing with boat-hooks ready to fend you off. We were adrift at the bottom of what seemed, in our small boat, a vast stone tank – Athlone lock is big enough to hold fifty-six closely parked cars – trying to throw a rope up a wall against the wind. The only thing to do was shout at the crew for his ineptitude, but the crew shouted back with a voice that can carry for many miles. We were barely speaking by the time we left the wretched place.

An hour later we were through the narrow channel between Coosan and Kilinure Point and into the calm of the inner lakes, still enveloped in a coating of ice. We headed for the only place where we knew we could tie up, and as the frost began to melt the dogs came out of hiding. This time we didn't need to be asked whether we wanted a reservation – the Wineport was to be the special treat of the holiday. That night we suffered no squeaky fenders, no dinghy banging against the hull (we had no dinghy). The only thing that woke me was thirst and the need for paracetamol.

Next morning we travelled north up the western shore of Lough Ree, cautiously following the beacons that marked the navigation channel. The weather was fine, which was important. We were nervous of Lough Ree, believing it to be less friendly than Lough Derg. It had more rocks, fewer harbours and was surrounded by flat land that made it open to any and every breath of wind.

The lake was said to have a monster. I was glad we'd conducted our ceremony before leaving home territory, as any monster would surely be in cahoots with Poseidon or his minions. Many lakes and bogs in Ireland have been feared after dusk for the creatures that live within them. The Shannon version, the *péist*, was said to be capable of tearing apart a fisherman's nets before towing him away to its lair.

There have been stories and rumours about Lough Ree for many decades, though perhaps not as many as those about Loch Ness in Scotland. The most reported Ree story comes from a trio of fishing priests. In May 1960, Fathers Quigley, Burke and Murray were on the Westmeath shoreline enjoying a quiet moment, when they spotted something unusual in the water. They described it as being long and narrow at the front with a pointed, serpent-like snout. This section of the creature was about 18 inches long and disappeared under the water. Further back a hump or loop rose up, the end of this putting the visible part at something like six feet, but they believed there was much more beneath the water. It moved smoothly without any form of undulation. They watched it for a few minutes, after which it gently submerged, surfacing again for another minute or two before disappearing for the last time. The local papers had a field day.

There are people who spend a good deal of time researching deep-water creatures, much as there are people who look for human-like hairy beasts such as the Himalayan Yeti or the North American Bigfoot. A researcher of 'sea serpents' is Jan Sundberg of GUST, the Swedish Global Underwater Search Team, who came to Ireland in June 2001 to research the Lough Ree sightings, the very time we were there ourselves! With him were Espen Samuelson of Norway and Nick Sucik, an American enthusiast who set up a website to document mystery animals worldwide. It was through Sucik that I came to know more about the Shannon monsters. I received an email from him in September 2003, which I thought at first was a hoax. He'd got in touch because I was webmaster of the Lough Derg branch of the Inland Waterways Association of Ireland (IWAI) and hoped I would have information. Correspondence showed him to be serious in his quest.

Sucik mentioned a sighting by a woman who lived near the lake and wondered if I knew her. I was surprised to find that I did. She was a fellow boater, a down-to-earth sailor, someone I thought most unlikely to imagine the fanciful. When her children were small, she would take them out rowing, and this was when she saw something in the water she could not explain. It was very large, and it made her so uneasy that she rowed hard for the shore. She still has no explanation for what she experienced.

We saw no sign of the researchers, and the researchers saw no sign of the monster: the GUST expedition to Lough Ree was a disappointment. They always are. Nobody can be sure whether this is due to a dearth of mystery animals, or because they are very shy, living only in the darkest, deepest parts of lakes that go down many fathoms. It's easy to explain them away as the result of wash from a boat or strange shadows on the water – the wash from a cruiser that passes on the other side of a lake can take fifteen minutes to reach the shore and can appear, when the light is just right, to be an animal, with the serpentine loops of many reported sightings. I rather hope we never find out; it gives an extra frisson to a trip out on the lake.

It was in the middle of Lough Ree that Aoife, the terrier, decided she didn't much like boating. We'd stopped overnight in Lecarrow halfway up the lake on the western shore, the village at the end of the small canal where we'd picked up weed in our hire boat. The canal was built in the 1840s, its original purpose to transport stone from a nearby quarry for the bridge and lock in Athlone. It was extended during the famine years to give employment, but silted up with the reduction of commercial traffic on the river. In 1966 it reopened to cater for the new breed of pleasure boater, providing a much-needed haven.

Lecarrow is very sheltered, and we'd awoken to a calm morning. When we poked our nose out into the lake it was a bit breezy but nothing too serious, so off we went, heading for Lanesborough. From the Lecarrow Canal you have first to go east across the lake, leaving Inchcleraun, a sizeable island, to your left or port side. Joe was at the wheel – he'd become adventurous on open water. We rounded Beacon 7 to turn north and the wind hit us. We were headed straight into it, which was good – at least there would be no broken crockery – but we were not happy. Neither was the small dog who jumped onto my lap, a dejected, shivering heap. Then she climbed over my shoulder and tried to get out of the boat. I caught her collar before she scuttled off down the narrow side deck or jumped ship, and held her tight on my knee.

The journey up the lake seemed endless. The sun went in and the water turned deepest black. The calmest among us was Frankie, the sheepdog, who remains unperturbed by everything but thunder and cracking sticks in the fire. We watched the chimneys of the Lancsborough power station approach, oh so slowly, but finally we were into the small lake below the bridge that joins Roscommon to Longford. I took the wheel and chugged into the old stone harbour, where we tied up and let the dogs off, giddy with relief. Aoife rolled and rolled on the grass then leaned against the stone wall and rubbed herself along it. A new trick.

Walking up the main street on the Longford side of the river, we saw a chandlers, so had to go in. The dogs came too. Inside we found something we'd heard of but not seen – buoyancy aids for dogs. Little orange jackets with a handle on the top that made them highly visible and allowed you to hoick them out of the water should they fall in. The dogs had a fitting and walked out dressed in neon. Aoife and Frankie were, we believed, among the first to wear such things, and they caused a bit of a stir. Passers-by and boaters would point and guffaw, but the dogs held their heads up high. They knew it wouldn't be long before any dog with a sense of fashion would have one.

Both of them had been overboard. Frankie was first. Earlier that year we'd anchored off Garrykennedy for a breakfast fry, and Frankie went for a mooch down the narrow side deck. Joe called her back in case she fell in, she tried to turn, lost her balance and toppled. She liked the water so didn't mind, but there was nowhere for her to get out. She swam round the boat a couple of times before Joe caught her collar with the boat-hook and hauled her out by the scruff of the neck. It's astonishing how much water a wet collie's coat can hold, and how efficient dogs are at shaking it out.

Another time we were rafted out – tied to the outside of another boat – and had to cross three or four vessels to reach the shore. Both dogs were jostling to follow Joe, Frankie squeaking with panic and frustration in her desperation to be first. Aoife was right behind and accelerated into an inside-overtake manoeuvre, giving Frankie her signature sideways nip on the way. Frankie took avoidance action and went swimming again.

Mostly it was Frankie who fell in, but sometimes Aoife would try to jump too wide a gap between boat and harbour wall, miss her footing and fall. This caused real panic as Aoife was Joe's little princess and he was sure she was drowning. The buoyancy aids helped keep us all calm while the dog was extricated.

Canine buoyancy aids are no longer an exclusive accessory – these days all the dogs on the river have them. Aoife wrecked hers scraping along the rough-hewn wall in every harbour we came to (the new trick had become a favourite occupation) and we had to get her a new one. Then we switched to harnesses as the dogs, especially Frankie, overheated in jackets. By 2009 Aoife was onto her third harness.

We made it to Rooskey, an achievement, I felt, as it took many hours of cruising time in our little boat. We stopped above the lock for cheese on toast and, as I opened the door of the oven, it emitted its usual painful, grating squeak. The small dog's tail went down between her legs. She'd had enough of this particular noise and hopped ashore. I called her back but she said, 'Won't' and stood her ground. Then she saw the pushchair. It was a three-wheeled affair with pointed bow and the ability to traverse the Rocky Mountains and it was coming towards us. The poor dog was having none of it and took off towards the lock. I jumped off the boat.

The pushchair kept on coming, its owner oblivious. We reached the lock, Aoife and I, with the monstrous vehicle behind. This was no stroller, it was a triple-wheeled horror from hell. The mother was fit and determined to exercise. A brief attempt to get her to stop failed. She looked at me with the bemused, exhausted, triumphant look of a new mother and kept on coming.

The dog ran past the lock and headed for the river with its strong currents. I ran after her, thinking the pushchair would surely stop here, but it didn't. I was becoming paranoid: this was no ordinary mother but a body that had been snatched or a Stepford wife. The real mother would shortly join our chase along the river bank, demanding the return of her child while the revealed alien floated to the space ship hovering invisibly over the water.

Aoife squeezed through a prickly gap in some bushes at the river's edge and refused to budge. The pushchair stopped, though I wasn't convinced. It could be a ruse. Peering into the bushes, I tried to coax Aoife out, but to no avail. I had to shrink myself between bushes and river to come at her from behind, grab her, shivering heap that she was, and take her back to the boat.

★★★

That summer, while on our adventure, we got three-foot-longer syndrome. It began gently and in the rain. *Caoimhe* was small and not very comfortable. At the rear was an open cockpit, which was delightful to sit in during fine weather when you could take down the canopy. With the canopy up you had to sit hunched forward, arms on knees, to avoid the sloping canvas, and inside the boat the seating was far from agreeable. You entered the saloon/galley from the cockpit. On the left were two bench seats with a table between in the arrangement commonly found on trains. The seats were too high and left your legs dangling, and the bench nearest the cockpit had a raised area in the middle to accommodate the engine. Sitting there was equivalent to having to sit at the plug end in the bath.

At the front of the boat was a V-berth (so called because it makes a V-shape), which in the daytime converted to seating. Here there were no dangling legs, but the curved wall of the hull made leaning back deeply uncomfortable. The windows steamed up at the slightest provocation. In bad weather you could end up with cabin fever, a crick in your back and loss of blood supply to the legs.

'We'll put in an advert and see what happens,' said Joe, and we started, quite casually, to look for another boat. We had thoughts of timber. This led to knowing smiles from anyone we told.

'A lot of work,' they'd say, shaking their heads.

We considered another Freeman. Perhaps the 26-foot version. We'd also had a fancy for twin engines since we saw the *Mary Francis*, a beautifully kept Freeman 33, turning in her own length inside a harbour, something you can do when you have two engines. We bought *Classic Boat* every month and looked with excitement at the brokerage pages, narrowing down the options to the boat builders we liked. We wanted an open cockpit as we enjoyed sitting outside, but this limited our choice – many boats have an aft cabin instead. We wanted a V-berth forward and comfortable seats down either side of the saloon. And lots of wood. We realised we would probably have to go to England to find something in wood – there were very few timber boats in Ireland, and even fewer for sale.

Joe put *Caoimhe* in the *Buy and Sell* in early summer. We couldn't do anything serious until we'd sold her, which was likely to take a while. We weren't even completely convinced we wanted to sell. We'd had the boat for less than a year. Could we justify buying another one so soon?

'I'd like to come and look at your Freeman,' said the man on the phone to Joe. 'I don't want to buy it. I just want to compare it to the one I'm going to buy.' This was our first (and only) enquirer. I was in the kitchen trying to piece together a conversation in which Joe's initial and obvious incredulity turned into a twenty-minute discussion about the qualities of Freeman boats, the merits of the River Barrow compared to the Shannon and the possibility of swapping our Freemans.

The man on the phone was Bobby Barden, and the following week he and his wife Pat drove down from Dublin to our marina in Cloondavaun Bay. They were in an open-top Saab whose push-button retracting roof Bobby enthusiastically demonstrated. He'd recently retired from a Saab dealership and had the car on loan.

'This is a much nicer boat than the one I'm buying,' said Bobby as we climbed aboard and set off into the lake.

'Would you like to drive?' I asked him once we

were out. Pat looked alarmed.

'Oh no. I'm happy sitting here.' Pat smiled in obvious relief and on we went.

'We could go to Terryglass for lunch,' said Joe. 'If you have time.'

'Are you sure?'

We liked Terryglass. It was half an hour across the lake with a sheltered harbour. The village was a short walk away and had two pubs, both of which served food. We chose the one next to the Post Office and went in.

'Let's have a proper lunch,' said Bobby happily as we settled at our table. 'My treat.' We protested.

'No no. You've let me come out in your boat. Will we have a bottle of wine? Red or white?' Pat gave him a look. By the time we were ready to leave for the harbour we were in fine spirits. We tucked Bobby and Pat into the seat at the back of the cockpit and set out for home.

'You know, I think I'm going to buy your boat,' said Bobby.

Chapter Four

*I*n November 2001 we walked through a scattering of low buildings towards the glitter of water beyond with its floating network of jetties. This was Parkstone Yacht Club in Poole, Dorset, and we were there to look at a boat. The jetties bounced and wobbled, the sound of our feet a dull thud as we turned off the main spine and onto a side rib. There it was, a Rampart 32, sitting quietly among chiming masts. She looked huge, her bow rising to the height of my shoulder and her side decks two feet above the walkway. It was November, but the sky was clear and blue. I tried to shut out the incessant talk of the owner, who was doing the salesman job. We were determined to be practical, to test whether each cruiser we saw fit the criteria we had set, but as I looked at this little ship I couldn't hold back the small bubble of excitement.

Burma Star was a motor cruiser constructed from timber – mahogany in the hull below and marine ply in the coach-house above. The hull was white, but the carvel planking showed through. The coach-house, with its angular aluminium 1960s windows, had recently been given a single coat of matching white, which didn't look good. The decks were pale blue. Our salesman told us the boat had been launched in 1969, one of the last to come out of the highly respected Rampart boat-yard in Southampton. The 1970s saw the rise and rise in popularity of the fibreglass cruiser: timber had had its day.

Parkstone Marina was extensive, the many berths sheltered from the Solent by man-made breakwaters. The people on the yacht next door were preparing to go to sea. They wore all the gear – bright red waterproofs from neck to dotey little sailing wellies – and were looking competent with lines and winches. *Burma Star* seemed to be the only non-sailing boat in the place. We noted her consequent lack of status by the looks of pity from our neighbours.

'Come aboard,' said the salesman owner, jumping on the aft deck ahead of us and gallantly holding out a hand to me. Up we climbed, marvelling at the way the boat held steady in the water. I peered into the cockpit. Lots of mahogany. A bit narrow. A proper instrument board with a light on a stalk you could bend around for night sailing (night sailing! Imagine!) Above your head as you stood at the wheel was another board of switches, all labelled: wipers; cockpit light; nav. lights; instruments. The floor was painted an ugly blue.

'There you go,' said the salesman opening the door to the saloon.

'Mind your head,' I said to Joe, an essential precautionary measure in *Caoimhe* – the scab on top of his head was generally fresh.

He didn't need to. He demonstrated the adequate height by straightening his back as he passed into the saloon. Compared to the tiny Freeman it was palatial. You could seat six people comfortably: three down each side. The upholstery was a royal blue with small dots of gold insignia and was, we were told, new. It looked it. A substantial ship's table was set between the seats. Highly varnished mahogany lockers (presses or cupboards to land people) were cleverly placed for maximum storage.

You could shut off the saloon from the rest of the boat with a door that closed – there were two cabins. On the right was the galley. A two-ring hob sat above a miniature fridge, half-size sink and drainer beside it. Behind was a short section of counter. It was just the thing for playing house (or boat). Opposite the galley was the bathroom (*heads* in sailing speak). Very exciting. *Caoimhe* had a walk-in locker containing a toilet on which, with careful manoeuvring, you could seat yourself. Here there was a toilet, a sink that pulled in and out from the wall on runners, a shower (the floor doubled as shower tray) and enough space for two people to turn round.

Finally, at the front of the boat was the fore cabin incorporating a V-berth – two bunks tapering into the pointy end of the boat – and a jolly board for linking the two together into something like a double bed so you could have jollies (contortionists only). It was all very satisfactory. I tried not to grin. I knew we'd found our boat.

★★★

Burma Star arrived in Ireland on the back of a lorry. I was anxious. Timber boats are vulnerable if not carried properly – planks can spring out of place if too much pressure is put on them and I had visions of high seas with lorry and boat piled up in a corner of the ferry, crushed. We'd booked her passage with a man from Banagher in Co. Offaly. He came highly recommended and appeared to know what he was doing, but you can never be sure. There was also her dignity to consider – how would she feel, exhibiting her nether regions as she travelled across two countries?

We'd arranged for the boat to be delivered to Eamon Egan's boatyard after travelling from Fishguard to Rosslare on the night ferry. It was December 21 and darkness came early. Our intention was to take *Burma Star* across Lough Derg to her berth in the marina an hour or so away, but this was dependent on her getting to Eamon's on time. There's a swing-bridge across the Shannon in Portumna, which opens for boats at set times. In winter there are only three – 09.45, 11.00 and 12.00. A ferry delay on the Irish Sea or heavy traffic on the road from Rosslare would scupper our plans.

At 10.30 a.m. we drove into the yard in a state of some agitation, but *Burma Star* was there before us, unharmed, on the back of the lorry. However, we were only part of the way through the ordeal – we now had to watch the terrible process of unloading. Eamon was, as always, unflustered and unhurried.

'She'll be grand,' he said as the broad webbing slings were passed under the hull and secured on the other side. This boat weighed over six tons and they were using webbing to hold it up? Good grief. I closed my eyes as the boat swayed in the flimsy cradle then turned my back, feigning nonchalance but fooling no one, until I judged she was safely lowered onto Eamon's trailer. This home-made device was hooked up to a tractor, which pulled the whole lot out of the boatyard, along the main road for maybe 100 metres, and down to the slip that would launch her into the Shannon. We walked alongside as the boat oscillated. It was pure torture.

There was a good deal of shouting and waving as the tractor reversed the trailer and its precious cargo down the narrow ramp towards the water. As *Burma Star* was lowered in, a cheer went up, but still I held my breath, not convinced that she had made her journey from England without a hitch. The slings were removed and there she was, restored to her own element, and just as lovely as we remembered her when last seen afloat in November.

Once again, the name had to go. We were making a habit of this. *Burma Star* didn't suit. I'm not sure I can explain why – it seemed like a name for a bigger boat, a rougher-built vessel, not a pretty timber craft with sweet lines like our new beloved. It's also the name of a British military award, not right for a boat on Irish waters. Much anguish comes with the process of choosing a new name, as you are going to have to live with it for the duration of your ownership. What's more it will be in the public domain. A favourite pastime for people sitting in a harbour is to watch and comment on other boats. A ridiculous name will cause derision. We'd already been through this with *Towed In A Hole* and had no wish to repeat the experience. On the drive to Eamon Egan's boatyard we were still without a name.

'It's a good day to be putting her into the Shannon,' I said. 'The Winter Solstice.'

'We could call her that,' said Joe.

St Stephen's Day 2001, and we were in Cloondavaun Bay Marina armed with a supply of sandpaper, paint stripper, scrapers of varying types and sizes and, on my part, six layers of clothing, much of it thermal. There was frost on the ground, but we couldn't wait to begin the job of removing the layer of white undercoat from the sides of the coach-house, so returning the boat to her timbered state. We scraped and I sweated inside my padding. The sun shone on our endeavours. There was not a soul about.

The timber beneath the paint was not in good condition. It was marine ply, not the mahogany of the rest of the boat, and had stains and discolourations, but we persevered. Over the years to come we would experiment with many different varnishes, and eventually, as a last (and mostly successful) attempt to make the timber look smart, Joe stained it dark and coated it with an epoxy resin that could be used in the cold and damp. In 2001 she was pale on her top, but we preferred it to the white paint and took her off into the lake with pride.

Manoeuvring *Winter Solstice* was like driving a Transit van through city streets after learning to drive

in a Mini. It wasn't just that she was 11 foot longer (so
much for three-foot-longer syndrome). She was, as a
fellow boater commented, a proper little ship, high in
the bow and heavy in the water with two engines. It
was good to practice in the off season with few people about to stare and snigger. We could cross the lake
to Terryglass for hot whiskey on a frozen blue-skied
day, or take a spin down to Dromaan or Dromineer if
we were feeling adventurous. I grew confident using
the twin engines and came to love the way I could
turn the boat in her own length: wheel hard down to,
say, the right, left-hand engine in forward, right-hand
engine in reverse and round we'd go. I had fellow
boater Mark Maguire to thank for the many tips he
gave when we did a short training day with him. Use
the same hand for both engines, he said – the temptation is to use left hand for port engine, right hand for
starboard, but somehow that gets the brain in a terrible spatial muddle.

He taught us 'man overboard' too, not an easy
manoeuvre, especially on a high-bowed boat where
you can't see the person – or fender – in the water.
We practiced on Lough Derg. The fender was thrown
over, 'Man overboard!', and I put *Winter Solstice* to turn
using engines and wheel. Joe was already on the bow,
pointing at the pretend person, pointing and pointing.
I came around to go head into the wind for maximum control of the boat and followed Joe's pointing.
He counted down the distance using his fingers – ten
fingers for ten feet and so on – and I stopped while he
leaned over with the boat hook. Missed. The fender,

luckily only a fender, floated past and I came around to try again.

Getting into a tight berth with two engines was a doddle compared to with one. No longer did I have to saw to and fro in the water, or even come at the space between boats on a harbour wall at a gentle angle – I could aim straight into the gap, Joe ready at the bow with the line, slowly, slowly until Joe signalled he had the rope round the cleat or bollard on the shore, then turn the wheel away from the wall, nudge forward against the tautly held rope, a spot of reverse, and in the stern would come, nice and tight.

★★★

As the days grew longer we went further, and planned a Big Summer Trip for July. Before the Big Trip, however, we decided to make our proper début at the Lough Derg Rally. This was – and is – the annual event organised by the Derg branch of the IWAI.

We'd snuck into this rally on *Caoimhe* the previous year, but in order to be properly part of it you had to buy into the full week – no trying it out for a day or so. We didn't know if we wanted to do this, so left *Caoimhe* in Dromaan Harbour where the rally was to begin and arrived at the boat on the starting day. It was raining and cold. We barely knew anyone. Having been asked if we had our 'rally pack' and answered no we hadn't registered, we were quickly rumbled. We went home.

In 2002 we were on our proper little ship and were unafraid of wind or rain, but *Winter Solstice* was still a very new toy. A rally with boatfuls of knowledgeable people seemed a good place to be. We knew a few of the other boaters and wanted to get to know more. We paid our money in advance.

The rally was to begin at our marina in Cloondavaun Bay. We arrived early and were given a large brown envelope containing details of all the activities and a number to stick in the cockpit window. The jollities lined up included boating competitions, line heaving, water sports, talent and ditty competitions, fancy dress, a table quiz and a treasure hunt. we were assured that you didn't have to take part in anything that didn't appeal. However, boats were put into teams of three, and points gained by their crews in the competitions were added to the team score. The culmination of all this was a dinner dance on the last night with prizes for event winners.

Rallies began on the Shannon in the 1950s during the early days of the IWAI, when the organisation's *raison d'être* was to keep the Navigation open. There were very few pleasure crafts on the inland waterways during the fifties, and as commercial traffic had all but ceased, the Shannon and Grand Canal were largely empty of boats. So much so that cruising the waterways for pleasure could cause deep suspicion. Seán MacBride, the former Chief of Staff of the IRA, Minister for External Affairs and Nobel Peace Prize winner, was an early campaigner for the waterways, having bought his first boat, a converted steam pilot called *Lady Di*, in the early 1930s, a time when the security forces still considered him a threat to the nation.

MacBride had taken his boat to Dublin on the Grand Canal for the winter, and on his return he describes being escorted by members of the Special Branch: 'They tried to make themselves inconspicuous, but they did not blend into the wilderness of the Bog of Allen.' On Lough Ree, MacBride was more difficult to observe, and Special Branch became convinced that his boat was a vital part of unspecified but subversive activities. In the early hours of one Sunday morning, the police boarded the boat they believed was his.

It was the wrong boat. Very badly the wrong boat as it happens, belonging as it did to Colonel Mansfield, a retired British Army colonel, on his modern yacht *Maureen*. To say Colonel Mansfield was indignant is an understatement. It was only later that MacBride, anchored that night in the inner lakes, heard of these events, when Colonel Mansfield visited *Lady Di* and invited him aboard *Maureen* for a drink.

By the 1950s, the Government could see little point in spending money on keeping the waterways navigable for the few boats that used them, so regularly put forward plans to close the canal or to hinder navigation on the Shannon by replacing lifting sections of bridges with fixed spans. Another ex-British Army officer, Harry Rice, was determined not to let this happen. In 1944, Harry returned to Athlone from India, having been invalided out of the Army, and he and his wife spent much of their time on the Shannon. Harry became an enthusiastic contributor of letters to the papers, sent in articles to the local press, wrote *Thanks for the Memory*, a book about navigating the Shannon and, perhaps most importantly, organised public protests whenever there was an attempt to build a new fixed bridge across the river.

The threat to the navigations of Ireland was so grave that a meeting was convened in order to set up the Inland Waterways Association. The inaugural meeting was on 7 January 1954 in the Shelbourne Hotel, and Harry Rice was elected president. The meeting adopted the following resolution:

> That this association is resolutely opposed to any attempt to amend the Shannon Navigation Acts so as to permit the obstruction of the Shannon Navigation, and, in particular, its obstruction by the erection of a fixed bridge at Athlone.

The Association believed it essential that the Shannon be made known to the public, many of whom had no idea of its value to tourism. The Shannon rallies became a way of promoting the river and its lakes.

In those days, boating people were tough and fearless. They went to rallies in open boats and brought tents or vans in which to sleep. The smaller cruisers did the same, tipping the children out at night to sleep under canvas. There were big competitions. Boat logs from 1964 and '68 recorded in *Silver River*, a collection of writings about the rally, include man overboard, fishing, navigation, timed trial course (guess how long it will take to get to …), inspection of cruisers and sailing. The modern-day Shannon Rally has all of these and more. There's swimming, rowing, boat handling, line heaving, a commando competition…. For the less active, you can fuss about with floral arrangements and fancy dress.

The Derg Rally had its fair share too. Our first event was the table quiz, but unfortunately I'm a liability on any quiz team, merely taking up space. It was held in the long back room of the Royal Shannon Hotel in Banagher, and we were teamed with Joe and Lana. Tables ran down one side of the room and mobile phones plugged into wall sockets ran down the other. I knew the answer to nothing.

Our second event, also in Banagher, was a treasure hunt. We roamed around the town and riverside picking up clues, happy we had some idea of what was expected of us, but we spent much of the rest of the week in a state of bewilderment. Most of the rally-goers had been on the water and rallying for years. They knew how to line heave, reverse in a figure of eight and write amusing ditties about rally people, boats and events.

One competition in which we *were* keen to take part was the boat rescue. You had to go alongside a boat that was feigning distress and tow it a set distance while being judged by an adjudicator. Joe had twisted awkwardly the night before while getting off the boat and was suffering with his back. He would be unable to deal with ropes, so we took on extra crew – someone who knew what he was doing. We were lurking in the bay at the end of the Scariff River waiting our turn when a call came on the VHF radio. It was from a boat we could see just across the water. 'We've broken down. Can you please help?' A real rescue! We swung into action and cruised to come alongside the small red sailing boat. My capable new crew member tied lines from fore to aft, designed to keep the distressed boat secure next to *Winter Solstice*. He explained that we should have a knife, or preferably an axe (!), at the ready. If the line from the bow became unattached, the stern could be pushed down and we would sink unless we cut the aft ropes immediately. We brought out the bread knife, having nothing else, and I spent the whole journey into harbour nervously eyeing our lines.

I glowed with pride at the way *Winter Solstice* conducted herself as we drove slowly towards Mountshannon, her two engines giving us both power and manocuvrability. We delivered our rescuee to a jetty, feeling pleased. We needed to go no further – this was tonight's destination, the last harbour of the rally, and the venue for the big prize-giving. A short while later, our team-mates Lana and Joe arrived, also with a boat attached. They too had been called on to do a real rescue of a hire boat that had run out of diesel. Our team would surely win a prize!

I enjoyed the dancing that evening, but prize-givings and speeches are an awkward form of entertainment, particularly when you're trapped at a dinner table. We didn't win anything. Not even for our team's dual rescue. Because it was real it didn't count. Pah!

Looking at photographs from the early rallies you can see that most of the boats were made from timber or steel. Fibreglass was a new material, yet to become the mainstay of boat construction. The boats were also low to the water. Indeed, their shape was still more or less the same at our first rally, pretty much all 'boat shaped' but for one exception, a fast fibreglass cruiser with facilities better than those in our house. We never dreamt that this type of boat would become the norm.

We went on the rallies for the next two years. The dogs loved it, especially Aoife, who'd always preferred the social life to being on the move, assuming as she did that the world was full of Aoife lovers. We learned to watch her closely after 'the incident' in 2003. We were in Portumna Castle Harbour, passing the time on a small trip boat that went from Portumna to Terryglass and back. We were distracted by chat and a glass of wine, so didn't realise our small dog had disappeared. It was Joe who spotted her trotting past, pork chop in mouth. It's impossible to catch a dog with a pork chop in its mouth.

What do you do when your dog steals someone's dinner? Confession seemed best, so we made shame-faced enquiries. Louis, the owner of the chop, was very good about it. The dog was unrepentant, the theft premeditated. Louis' boat was moored with the bow to the harbour wall, so was not easy to access. Aoife hopped on board, trotted along the deck, found her way through the cockpit and saloon to the galley and stole the chop.

★★★

The first time it happened we were cruising up Lough Ree on a calm, sunny day. We'd spent the night in Lecarrow and were heading to Lanesborough at the top of the lake. It was calm, unlike the last time, which was a relief for the small dog (and us). We had owned *Winter Solstice* for just six months and were getting to know her quirks. The rally had helped, but there was so much more to learn than on little *Caoimhe*. We had our eyes set on the north Shannon, a journey that would introduce us to many new reaches of the river.

As we left the Lecarrow Canal and crossed Blackbrink Bay, I checked the gauges (mostly so I could answer yes when Joe barked 'Have you checked the gauges?') Unlike *Caoimhe*, *Winter Solstice* had gauges for all sorts of things – engine temperature, engine oil pressure, gearbox oil pressure, engine revs, battery charging. The little dial on the starboard engine temperature gauge was way up. I yelped.

'We're overheating on the right!' Joe leaned out of the back to see if water was spurting from the exhaust. It wasn't.

'Turn it off!' *Winter Solstice* gave a small shudder as I pulled the off switch. Then I pulled the other off switch just to make sure. There was silence as we drifted.

Nicki Griffin

'What did you do that for?! Start it up again!' The word 'stupid' hung in the air.

It was fortunate that we had a second engine. However, we didn't know if it would be any use without the first. Many twin-engined boats refuse to travel in a straight line on one motor. On a single-engined boat, the propeller sits beneath the stern halfway between one side and the other. On a twin-engined boat like ours, there are two propellers, one on the right and one on the left. When you engage the left-hand engine, the boat is pushed to the right. When you engage the right-hand engine, the boat is pushed to the left. The steering wheel turns the boat in a predictable way as in a car.

On a boat with only the left-hand engine working, the way to counteract the thrust of the engine pushing the boat to the right is to turn the steering wheel all the way to the left. On some boats this works. On others it doesn't. I imagined us trapped on Lough Ree in perpetuity, circling like a whirligig beetle on a pond, ignored by passing boats. I turned the steering wheel hard to the left and engaged the port (left-hand) engine. The boat staggered along in something approaching a straight line.

We knew *Winter Solstice* had something called bilge keels, and had seen them when she arrived on the lorry, but hadn't realised how useful they were. These little timber side fins are in addition to the main keel that runs down the centre of the hull, and are there to give the boat more stability – they make it roll less. The main keel, the ridge running down the centre of the hull, helps a boat to travel in a straight line instead of sliding sideways with the wind or current, and *Winter Solstice* had a deep, sharp-nosed one. The combination of the bilge keels and the deep, narrow main keel gave us purchase on the water, enabling steerage on only one engine.

Just north of Lecarrow is a small harbour called Portrunny, where I aimed the boat at an old wooden jetty poking out from the shoreline, its timbers half rotten. There was a straggle of houses and a lifeless pub. The clouds sat low over the lake. I didn't relish the idea of being stranded here, but I relished even less the idea of not being able to land. *Winter Solstice* approached the jetty in a straight line, but as soon as I eased the engine back she went right. I turned the wheel full to the left but still she went right.

'What are you doing?' cried Joe.

'She won't go in.'

'For fuck's sake…'

I came around in a circle and aimed for the jetty again. Joe was up at the bow with a rope. It was a high jetty, but I brought the bow close enough for him to clamber onto the dodgy-looking timbers. The stern began to drift out, but I was powerless to bring it in without the starboard engine.

'Throw me a rope can't you?' bawled Joe. I scrambled onto the aft deck and did as my dear husband requested. He caught it, thank God.

Joe took up the floor panel to reveal the starboard engine, got onto his knees and started poking about. Something was clearly blocked. I took the dogs for a walk so I could sulk in peace. When I returned, Joe held up a metal object in triumph. It was the cylindrical weed trap pulled from the bowels of *Winter Solstice*.

'There we are.' It was packed with vegetation.

Chapter Five

*W*hen the floating pontoon sank into the water, the event was pronounced a success. The weight of people was at least equal to that of the previous year. As water lapped around our toes, Joe and I looked at each other, bemused. We had barely stepped onto the jetty when we were told 'You need to get a glass for your Harvey Wallbanger'. Now, on this sinking pontoon, we were drinking the orange liquid.

We'd heard about Acres Lake while at the Lough Derg Rally – tens of boats travelled there each July, the more musical occupants attending the Joe Mooney Summer School of traditional Irish music in the Co. Leitrim town of Drumshanbo. Acres Lake was a bulge in the Lough Allen Canal with a few appealing facilities such as a small but heated outdoor pool and a couple of tennis courts. The children would go to classes with their fiddles and flutes and banjos, or swim and play games, and the adults would sit in the sun and gossip between boats.

We'd made good time from Lough Ree to this northernmost part of the Shannon Navigation, which was something of a surprise. A blockage in the weed trap was nothing to the engine problems we experienced on the way. But here we were chugging out of the narrow canal into the little lake.

'Good grief,' I said. We could only assume there were jetties in there somewhere. Boats were tied to boats that were tied to boats. They were sideways on and end on and tucked in backwards. Where could we possibly go? I stopped *Winter Solstice*. Surely, having come all this way, we would find somewhere. As we hovered, a figure on a barge noticed us and waved. The Lough Derg branch of the IWAI was here. We were to go round the back.

It seems to be a general rule that men on barges cannot resist a boating challenge, particularly when it involves ropes. Soon we had advisers on all sides as I inched between many feet of heavy metal, then passed our lines to waiting hands to be tied onto a boat that was tied to a boat that was tied to a boat.

Disembarkation was going to be tricky – we'd have to climb over the pulpit with two dogs. The pulpit on a boat, although a splendid place from which to give a sermon, has a different purpose – it's a safety rail that rises from the deck at the bow and extends around it. We passed the dogs between the rails and transferred them to the back of the craft next door. From there, the four of us climbed onto the side deck of a cruiser, and then down to the bathing platform that jutted at water level from a small Dutch cruiser. Up the steps, across the deck and onto the jetty to be told we needed glasses (which were on the boat) for the Harvey Wallbangers. What?

It was a tradition, we were told, and was provided each year by Cormac Kenny.

This drink, for those not up on their cocktails, is a mixture of vodka, orange juice and Galliano. I thought Galliano was just a very yellow cocktail ingredient in a tall bottle but no! According to the Galliano website, it is:

> ... all that is great about Italy. A love of authentic craftsmanship combined with flair and imagination. A belief in doing things the right way, never cutting corners. Respect for heritage and tradition, but also embracing the future with open arms. A vivacity, a smile – 'un sorriso' – and a love of life. Galliano is 'Spirito Italiano'.

A lot of responsibility for a cocktail component to carry! The classic Harvey Wallbanger recipe is five parts orange juice, two parts vodka and one part Galliano. Vodka, orange juice and ice are mixed in a glass and the Galliano is floated on the top. Frilly bits such as tiny umbrellas and slices of fruit give it that decadent cocktail appearance. I don't know what proportions were used at Acres Lake that evening, but there were no frilly bits and the Galliano was not floated. White plastic pails resembling the containers that hold catering mayonnaise appeared at regular intervals from *76M*, Cormac Kenny's barge, providing top-ups for every empty glass. There was no ice.

Leaking diesel had been an ongoing problem since Lough Ree, and the stink of it had impregnated the timbers of the boat. Removing diesel was a deeply disagreeable job, especially when all you had was a bucket, home-made scoops and a sponge. Joe decided that changing the oil filters might stop future leaks, but he had no new ones. Chat among the men found Johnny, who had a car parked nearby, enjoyed engine stuff and was prepared to drive around local garages. Filters were found, and Joe spent a messy few hours on a job that required unusual contortions of head and arm. I kept out of the way.

The Joe Mooney Summer School finished, groups of boats were going their separate ways, and we kept our fingers crossed the diesel would stay where it belonged. The barges of the recently formed Heritage Boat Association (HBA), many of whom we'd met on Lough Derg, were going up the last stretch of the Lough Allen Canal and into Lough Allen itself. This big open lake had two harbours, but only Spencer Harbour was attached to the land, so this was their destination. We decided to go with them. After interminable manoeuvring of barges along the shallow canal and through the Drumshanbo Lock, we finally cruised onto the lake ourselves, playing catch-up with the big boats. In the distance was a growing clot of barges as one became two became three became four. Finally seven were tied together to form a giant raft. A terrace of metal with people strolling from houseboat to houseboat.

Lough Allen is as far as you can go on the Shannon – the Navigation ends at the north-eastern tip of the lake just above Inishmagrath Island, the suddenly small

Shannon flowing into the lake from its source in the Cuilcagh Mountains. As with any major river, there is an ancient legend that explains how it was born: the Shannon was created out of Connla's Well, the source of all wisdom in ancient Ireland. Connla's Well, surrounded by nine hazel trees and guarded by cup-bearers who administered the Waters of Wisdom, was out of bounds to women. But wouldn't you know, one of them got it into her dizzy head she wanted this forbidden knowledge. Sinann, granddaughter of Ler, sealord of the *Tuatha Dé Danann*, ancient people of Ireland, wanted this knowledge so badly that one day she decided she'd had enough and strode off up to the well, evading the cup-bearers who guarded it so tightly. She got her comeuppance of course, audacious woman – the well erupted, washing her away in its giant flood. However, this was fortunate for us boaters, as the mass overflow of water became the River Shannon, named after the woman who was not content with beauty and domestic duties. Same old story: woman as temptress, source of the downfall of men, seeker of forbidden knowledge and cause of subsequent mayhem. As a river, the female continues to threaten upset with its floods and moon-caused tides.

Lough Allen was the end of the holiday for many members of the HBA. We, however, had another glorious week on our still-new boat. We would go to Lough Key. Travelling south from Acres Lake you pass through Carrick-on-Shannon then come to a fork in the river. If you bear right you enter the Boyle River, a twisting, tree-lined navigation that takes you through Cootehall in Co. Roscommon, up a level at Clarendon Lock and into the beautiful, island-dotted Lough Key. It was after Cootehall that we realised the bilges were once more full of diesel, and the boat was limping, struggling along with low oil pressure.

At Clarendon Lock we paused to study the chart. There were three public moorings, all of which were in Lough Key Forest Park, the old demesne of Rockingham that was established as a park in 1972. Joe examined the options through binoculars as we came closer. We could see two of the jetties and both looked isolated and lonesome with not another boat for company. We weren't in the mood for lonesome with our engine malfunctioning. That left the main quay wall.

'There's a Navigation notice,' said Joe, peering at the chart. 'It says "Rockingham jetties exposed in north-west to north-east winds. Use Drumman's Island jetty in these conditions." Where's the wind coming from?' I didn't know, but it was brisk enough to send choppy little waves across the water in front of us. We motored on, looking anxiously ahead. We couldn't see another jetty. Perhaps the chart was out of date and it was no longer there. We were re-imagining our plans, when a line of boats came into view. No. Two lines. The Rockingham jetty had cruisers moored two abreast along the whole length. With a depressing feeling of *déjà vu*, we lingered for a moment, then realised we recognised the boats from Acres Lake.

There is often an awkward moment when a strange boat arrives and clearly would like to raft to the boats already in place. If it's nearly dark or the weather's bad, it would be a churlish and thoughtless skipper who would turn a boat away, but it was the middle of the day. There was a bit of wind, but this wasn't Lough Derg or Lough Ree. We had the choice of two other jetties on the lake. These boats had travelled together from Acres Lake, so we were outsiders again. But we really didn't want to have to turn back with the boat in such sickly condition. We lingered awhile.

Finally, and with understandable reluctance, we were invited to come alongside a boat. It was Johnny from Acres Lake, who'd driven Joe around the countryside to find the correct oil filters.

'We're only planning to stop for a few hours to sort out the engine problem,' we told him. Our boat rocked vigorously in the north-east wind at the aptly named Rockingham as we considered what to do next.

There is a certain type of man (and it is almost invariably a man) who is happiest when tinkering with something mechanical. He does not settle well to long family days of relaxation, chat and 'fun'. This type of person is invaluable when you arrive into a harbour with diesel in your bilges and no idea why.

The oil filters tracked down at Acres Lake made no difference at all. In fact, as Joe discovered when we returned home, new filters had already been fitted by the mechanic who'd serviced the engines. It became clear we'd be stopping at Rockingham for rather more than a few hours. The tinkerers set to work: Johnny and Tony hopped into the cockpit where the covers were already off the engines. Joe was on hand to do whatever he could. I would either be trapped in the saloon having to listen to engine talk, or out on the quay in weather that wasn't warm enough to sit out in.

'I'm taking the dogs for a walk,' I said to Joe's back.

'OK.' I could have said I was going up in a hot air balloon and he'd have said OK in the same distracted voice. I gathered up the dog leads while Aoife barked hysterically and set off up the grassy bank towards the woods. We followed a path that took us along the edge of the lake, the dogs' feet making hollow thuds as they galloped. There was an avenue of russet-barked trees with enormous girth. Some branches, the size of trees themselves, had fallen but continued to grow, bending upwards towards the light. Dinosaur trees. I stood at the apex of a stone humpback bridge that crossed a lilied canal. The walls were decorated with rocks of strange and twisted shapes. I'd walked into a land of dreams.

There are three canals in the Forest Park, a telling reminder of the way things were when Rockingham was the estate of one of the biggest landowners in Ireland. It belonged to the King family, known variously as Earls of Kingston and Lords Lorton. Rockingham combined beauty and utility to produce an extraordinary, enchanted environment. The lily-filled canals were not only pleasant for ladies and gentlemen to stroll beside on a summer's day, they also transported goods to the house. The canal in the north east of the property was used to bring turf from the neighbouring bog. The turf boat was unloaded out of sight of the upstairs inhabitants, and taken via an underground passage to the domestic quarters. In a similar vein, the domestic offices were sunk below ground level to avoid obstructing the view across lawns to the park. The owners could maintain the illusion of a place where the mundanities of life did not occur.

Before the lands were given to the King family, Rockingham was the stronghold of the MacDermots: in those days it was called Moylurg. In the bay, within easy rowing distance of the boat quay, is a small island on which stands a fantastical but burned-out folly castle. It is known today as Castle Island, but in the time of the MacDermot clan it was simply The Rock. The MacDermot castle was not the whimsy of latter years, but a major fortress which made frequent appearances in the *Annals of Lough Cé*, a chronicle of Irish affairs from 1014 to 1590. The *Annals* report a good deal of fighting, even more partying and, according to the present-day Clan MacDermot, chess playing.

As you would expect, there is a legend about the MacDermots of Moylurg. It's of the unrequited love variety, much appreciated by balladeers, in which the beautiful daughter falls in love with the honest and handsome but not-wealthy-enough neighbour. Úna Bhán, the golden-haired daughter, was forbidden by her father to see Tomás Láidir, the handsome neighbour, and she steadily faded away in her despair. The father relented but, as in all good tragedies, he left it

too late (honour/stubbornness and so on) and Úna
Bhán died of a broken heart. She was buried on Trinity
Island in Lough Key to where the grieving Tomás
Láidir swam every night to sit at her grave. Eventually
he caught pneumonia and died, and was buried at her
side by her repentant father. The two were together
at last, which was of little use to anyone but made a
satisfactory ending to the story.

The MacDermots were kings of Moylurg from
around 1185 until the mid seventeenth century, and
for most of that time they inhabited a number of incar-
nations of the castle on The Rock. They were great
patrons – under their patronage the Cistercian monastery Boyle Abbey was founded in the twelfth century
and the *Annals of Lough Cé* were written. However, by
the seventeenth century their days as kings of Moylurg
were over. In 1603, Sir John King was granted a lease
of Boyle Abbey by Elizabeth I, and in 1667 his son Sir
Robert King was granted the lands that had belonged
to the MacDermots.

A later Robert King built a new house on the
banks of Lough Key in 1810, a magnificent mansion
designed by John Nash, the architect responsible for
Regent's Park and Regent Street in London. L.T.C.
Rolt, writer of many books about boating and the
waterways, visited the house when cruising round
Ireland with his wife in 1946. There were few boats
on the inland waterways in this post-war year of fuel
shortages, so they had the place to themselves. They
dropped anchor in the bay of Drumman's Island and
were entranced by the lake, parkland and woods. The

owner at the time was Sir Cecil Stafford King-Harman (marriages having expanded the original name), who offered them a bath and dinner. Rolt described the house as

>...an urban mansion set in the wilds of Connaught; it has an arrogance which is incapable of any concession to its surroundings.

However, he also believed it to be the best example of Nash's country houses. Alas, it is no longer possible to judge, as the house burned down in 1957 and was subsequently demolished.

After the fire the King-Harmans never returned to Rockingham, and in 1959 the estate was put up for sale. It was not a good time to sell, but eventually the Land Commission bought the land, first giving grazing rights to local farmers, then dividing the farm lands between them. This left 350 hectares of forest and parkland, which in 1972 became Lough Key Forest Park.

Sir Stafford King-Harman may have been very hospitable to the Rolts, but he was still a landlord and a member of the Anglo-Irish aristocracy. Not everyone was given a bath and dinner, or even permission to drop anchor in a bay of the lake. By 1955 there was a notice at Clarendon Lock on the approach to Lough Key stating it was prohibited to land on the shore or on the islands of the lake. No doubt it depended on the cut of your jib and the sound of your voice whether you were allowed to stay.

This was probably not much of an issue when there were few pleasure crafts on the river, but as leisure boating became more popular, there were those who resented this prohibition, believing the lake should be open to all. In 1955, Harry Rice travelled to Lough Key with a small flotilla as part of his ongoing campaign to keep canals and rivers open to boats through drawing attention to their beauty, to the need for essential repairs to the waterways' infrastructure and, in this case, to claim the right of ordinary people to enjoy the glories of Lough Key and its shores.

When I arrived back at the boat after my walk through the woods, I found there had been a diagnosis on *Winter Solstice*. One of her engines needed a new olive. This is something metal that resembles an edible olive and stops noxious liquids leaking into the bilges. It is, I am told, a compression-type sealer.

The olive was fitted, but Lough Key casts a spell over those who pause there, making it difficult to leave. We stayed for five days, steadily inching our way into the pack of boats until we were tied against the quay wall. After three days the wind dropped, and I missed it rocking us to sleep at night. We had become accustomed to the creak of ropes, to judging the sway of the deck before we stepped on board and to the slight frisson of danger. After all, we were going against the advice of the chart. What brave sailors we had become now we were not alone.

One evening I took the dogs up the hill behind the run-down and closed restaurant to the Moylurg Tower, an eye-catching structure that stands on the site of the old house. Its concrete walls are streaked and stained. Its architectural style is 1970s brutalist car park. The jutting balconies, from which you can view the surrounding countryside, resemble an unfinished lift shaft. It does not smell of urine, but you wouldn't be surprised if it did.

On returning to the boat, I discovered a barrier had gone up between me and it. A six-foot fence, made from the meshed panels you find guarding a building site, was being raised by uniformed men.

'What's going on?' I said.

'Private event tomorrow. This area's closed to the public.'

'But I need to get to my boat.' The workman looked at me doubtfully.

'We weren't told about that.'

I slid down the bank to the quay wall and found a gap at the bottom.

The following morning we awoke to further activity and settled back to monitor proceedings. A man in a white van erected his bouncy castle. Caterers arrived to bring the restaurant back to life. Every so often scouts were sent out from our camp to check progress and report back. They discovered that MBNA, the big credit card bank with offices in Carrick-on-Shannon, was having a hooley for its staff and their families. The bank had 450 employees in Carrick. Approaching 2,000 people would be causing a diversion that afternoon, and we were not invited.

Two men with clipboards crabbed down the bank towards us, looking for whoever was in charge. A group gathered on the quay to receive them.

'You'll need to move from here. This is a private event.'

'And this is a public harbour. You can't move us.' Hands were metaphorically rubbed as self-righteous indignation filtered through the boats. More people stepped onto the quay.

'They say we have to move.'

'They can't do that. They have no right.'

'We're not feckin' moving. Just let 'em try and make us.'

The clipboards retreated. A while later they returned.

'OK you can stay…'

'Of course we can stay. It's a public harbour.'

'… but you'll have to stay down here on your boats. You can't be wandering around. It's a private party.'

'We have to walk the dogs. You can't stop us doing that.'

'You've no right to …'

The clipboards retreated.

'So when do they start the food?' said someone.

Around lunchtime, a trickle then a deluge of families arrived to provide the afternoon's entertainment. Joe and I perched atop *Winter Solstice* in the sunshine and watched children roaring round full of ice-cream and excitement while knots of adults sat in the sunshine, happy with a day out on the company. As evening fell we could smell the smoke of barbecues. It was easy to mingle with the jolly crowd, and join the queue for the burgers and steaks and salads. I did draw the line, however, at going back for seconds. I'm a wimp at blagging and gatecrashing, not out of principle, but because I am afraid of being told off.

The Rockingham demesne was used to playing host to grand events. In 1862 the Hon. Robert King put on a sailing regatta on Lough Key. He had a new boat, *Meta*, which won the first two races. However, as Ruth Delaney in *The Shannon Navigation* suggests, the regatta was probably more of a social occasion for the gentry and a day out for the locals than a major competition – there were very few yachts racing on the Shannon during the 1860s. Later, during Sir Cecil King-Harman's time, there was an annual pheasant shoot on the estate followed by a Grand Ball. The British Ambassador came, along with the Anglo-Irish gentry from miles around and a variety of local dignitaries. Local children were kept from school for this great Rockingham event. The boys were employed as beaters while the girls and their mothers did the cleaning and catering.

Not everyone approved of the King-Harmans or their predecessors. John McGahern, the celebrated Irish writer, lived in Cootehall during the 1940s and early '50s – his father was sergeant at the local police barracks. For a while he was schooled by Master Kelly in Knockvicar alongside the children from Rockingham. He reports how Kelly, a rabid republican, gave these children a hard time, particularly after the annual shoot, which would put him into a rage. 'The peasants are still beating the pheasants out of the bushes for Milords,' he would say. He would give the Rockingham children a test for which they were not prepared, then beat them when they inevitably performed badly – 'a blow for every error or unanswered question.'

★★★

We returned to Lough Derg at the end of the summer, and realised we would have to find a new berth. Our allocated pontoon was too short even for *Caoimhe* at 23 ft, so it was no use at all for *Winter Solstice*. During the winter we'd borrowed the mooring of a boat that had been lifted, but by summer we were moving from one place to another. There was a shortage of berths on the lake – everyone seemed to be buying boats – so we were getting worried. However, Joe is a specialist at nosing things out and asking people for help or favours or information. Halfway down the lake in Williamstown, right next to our old friend Angus Leavie and Shannon Castle Line, was a little cut-out harbour with a splendid barge called *Jarrow* living in it. There was also space for another boat. Joe got on the phone, and within days we had a new place to park.

Chapter Six

*I*t was time to explore waterways other than the Shannon, and our opportunity came during the Easter weekend of 2003. Brian Goggin, a member of the IWAI, was to lead a 'canal virgins' adventure up the Grand Canal. There would be enough boaters with experience of locks to encourage those of us afraid of setting out alone on this under-used waterway. The 132-km Grand Canal connects Dublin with the River Shannon, passing through the peat bogs of the Midlands, and has never been as popular as the Shannon with its lakes, public harbours and pretty villages. Shannon boaters (ourselves included) tended to be anxious about managing the locks, and canal weed getting tangled in the propeller.

The journey began in apprehension and excitement at Shannon Harbour on the eve of Good Friday. In 2000 we'd stopped below the lock that joined river to canal – any further was out of bounds on our hire boat – but this time we kept going, lock-keeper Jason helping us up through two locks into the main basin of the harbour. We found a dozen other boats gathered, their crews a mix of experience and ignorance.

'That's a fine bargepole,' someone we didn't know commented as we tied *Winter Solstice* to another boat. We weren't sure if they were being serious. Ours was, indeed, a fine bargepole, but not very straight, having been cut from a hedge only the day before – a stout length of ash nearly as long as the coach-house roof. We also had, as instructed by Brian, a boarding plank (made by attaching timber to an aluminium ladder), two strong metal stakes and a lump hammer.

On Good Friday morning we woke to sunshine and optimism. We were given instructions and advice at the skippers' briefing before setting out in batches for the day's first lock. Its keepers were on alert that novices were on the way. There was uncertainty in our small camp about how *Winter Solstice* would do. We'd been told it was not advisable to take a twin-engined boat along the canal. The depth was good enough – supposedly four feet, although that depended on factors such as rainfall – but we had two propellers. There had a been a few sharp intakes of breath. Shaking heads suggested we would damage the props on the banks of the canal, or they would pick up too much weed or plastic bags or other rubbish. However, we were (mostly) confident. *Winter Solstice* had a beam of only 9 ft 6 in and the props were tucked up neatly into her buttocks.

The first lock at Clononey Bridge was a short stretch from Shannon Harbour, and we made it that far without mishap. We were reliant on others to open the lock gates for us, not only because we hadn't a clue, but because we didn't have a lock key, an essential piece of equipment to allow water in and out of the lock chamber. We virgins had all ordered our keys from Waterways Ireland, but they had to be manufactured and some wouldn't be available until we arrived in Lowtown at the end of our Easter trip. This wasn't as foolish as it sounds – there were plenty of people with lock keys to let us through on the way up, but on our return we would very likely need to do the job ourselves.

The Grand Canal rises from the Shannon through the Midlands before dropping again towards Dublin, so we would be going uphill for the first half of our journey, the locks acting as 'steps'. We had to wait our turn for the lock, and were told we'd be going in with another boat to save time and water – whenever a lock is filled and emptied, the upper level loses water. The more boats go through, the more the levels drop, causing problems for those with a bigger draught. *Winter Solstice* was going in first so at the signal I steered her out from the bank. The opening into the lock was narrow, dark and uninviting. We edged through the tail gates (on the lower 'step') into the crypt-like space, and I put the boat into reverse to stop. Joe was already on the bow ready to sling a line to Jason, who passed it round a hefty bollard and lowered it back to Joe.

My turn to throw a rope from the stern – not as easy as it sounds when you're balanced on the aft deck and there's many eyes watching. Third time lucky and I was clutching my end of the line. Unlike in the locks of the previous day, I had plenty of time to examine our dungeon as we waited for the second boat to edge in behind us. The walls were green and dank. Water dripped. It smelled of the underworld. I swallowed claustrophobia as our companion boat chugged in. Joe decided we should swap places – he thought he'd do better at fending off behind. It wasn't so bad once I was on the bow – more light, less prison-like, but even so I was very close to the heavy timber breast gates. I peered over the bow and could see the cill at their base, a concrete ledge we'd been warned about – not a problem when going up but a boat could get caught on it going down. I was anxious about the cill.

The tailgates closed, trapping us in a slimy stone chamber with no escape ladders – the only way out was to climb the lock gates. Jason appeared on the footboard of the breast gate, fitted his lock key onto the spindle that controls the racks and began cranking. I watched the rack ease up, the sluice open and water pour in and in and in. *Winter Solstice* rocked from side to side. Jason opened the second rack. Water boiled beneath the bow, and I stepped back as it threatened to splash over the deck, clinging to my surging rope. We rose in a bath of turbulence until the chamber was full. A new country revealed itself, the lock gates opened and we were free.

It was strange negotiating a narrow channel after the forgiving width of the Shannon. I found the boat drifting towards one bank or the other if I took my eyes off the road for a moment, and there were lilies and weeds that made me nervous. Would they catch in the prop, or block the engine if I ran over them? We travelled slowly to avoid damage to the banks from our bow wave, and because putting on speed would cause the stern to dig into the water with a risk of hitting bottom. I found myself soothed by the steady rhythm and relative quiet of the engines. Willow warblers were in full song in the hedges lining the towpath, the falling trill of notes growing and fading as we passed along. Primroses and cowslips blossomed everywhere. I hadn't seen so many cowslips since I was a child – they grew along the towpaths of the Shropshire Union Canal in the Cheshire countryside where I used to play. A canal that seems so very narrow whenever I return. The boats that still chug across the aqueduct next to my Nantwich secondary school are only 7 ft wide. The locks are barely any wider – you feel you could cross them in one stride – but very long, allowing a maximum narrowboat length of 72 ft. The Irish canal locks are twice the width but a little shorter, taking a boat of 61 ft x 13 ft.

We paused at Belmont for lunch, where giant bollards, painted white with black tops, strode through the cowslips on the bank. These bollards were designed to take a fully laden canal boat with no mechanical way of stopping – barges with Bolinder engines and no reverse. Using a rope slung round the bollard was the only way to prevent them crashing into the lock gates. Slinging our own ropes round these fat posts was a different proposition to popping a line round the delicate cleats on the jetties of the Shannon, and as we closed we could see there would be a gap between boat and bank – the canal shallowed out at the edge.

'Throw us your bow rope!' someone shouted from the bank.

'And your aft!' said another. We did both, and I switched off the engines, concerned about the prop on that shallow edge. We were pulled silently towards the bank, then abruptly stopped.

'Are we aground?' I gasped.

'Don't worry,' said a non-canal virgin. 'That's what your bargepole for.' I tried not to think about how we'd cope on our own. Someone would have to get ashore with a line, I thought, and that could mean a three- or four-foot jump.

Winter Solstice was as close to the bank as we could get her. Time to try out our boarding plank. It was lying on the coach-house roof, so Joe and I each took an end then shuffled along the side deck like old men in slippers. Once at the corner with the aft deck, we paused, thinking what to do next.

'Let me take it,' said Joe, so I let go and he heaved it into place. The metal rungs stretched beyond the bollards onto the tow path, but it joined the boat to the land and I ran down it while Joe freed the dogs from the saloon. They weren't nearly as impressed with the boarding plank as we were, impatient of its length, jumping on and off part way along.

So far, so good. I felt pleased with ourselves as I opened the tiny fridge to take out a collection of little packages: Parma ham, Brie and mature Irish Cheddar, olives, cherry tomatoes, green salad from the garden and some good bread. To complete the decadent feel, we opened a bottle of chilled white wine, squeezed into the already full fridge. After that I felt ready for any type of lock.

Except for this one. It was a double. On the canals in Cheshire a double lock took two boats in parallel. Not so here – the Belmont lock was two locks in series. We were told we'd have plenty of help and there was nothing to fear. The effusive reassurance made me anxious.

We were first in again, another cruiser squashing in behind.

'Use each end of your bargepole to fend off from the wall,' Brian said. Necessary advice, as only an aft line attached us to the bank – the fore section of the boat was under the bridge and free from constraint. I had the bargepole job and sat staring in dismay, the pole balanced across my lap, at the second lock chamber before me, Alan on the breast gate footboard opening the racks. The gentle waterfall became a torrent, formed into a wave and reared up to race towards me. The boat was pulled first to one side then the other by turbulence. I fended off, but the push of water was too unpredictable. There was shouting from the aft deck.

We had to do it all over again in the second chamber, but this time there was less frothing water and we had proper support from a line fore and aft. Relief of daylight as we rose. Volunteers from waiting boats were leaning on the balance beams ready to use their weight against them to push the lock gates open.

Crossing the Midland bogs the following day, we could see smoke up ahead. Reports filtered through from those who had radios that wildfires were burning through the gorse and peat, and in some places flames had leapt the canal. When I heard that even *The New York Times* had reported the fires I felt a ridiculous sense of importance, guiltily thrilled at the possible danger even as I thought about all that timber beneath me, and the untold damage to wildlife and the atmosphere.

There's a lot of bog in Ireland. In fact only Finland, Canada and Indonesia have a higher percentage of this black spongy stuff. In Ireland, 16.2 per cent of the land mass is made up of peatlands. And there isn't just one type of bog-standard bog – we have blanket bog, fen (a kind of pre-bog) and raised bog. In the Midlands it's raised bog, although you wouldn't know it by looking at it. These bogs have been drained and harvested over the last 400 years, leaving them as black deserts where the rich flora and fauna found in untouched bogs has long disappeared.

For a bog of any type to form, there must be high rainfall, a continuous growth of vegetation, poor drainage and a low level or absence of oxygen in the waterlogged soil. About 13,000 years ago, the land in the Midlands had all these qualities. After the last Ice Age the glaciers retreated, leaving behind hills and bumps (eskers, moraines and drumlins) and the hollows in between. These badly drained hollows filled with water, plants began to grow, every year partially decaying to leave a deposit of peat at the bottom. As the climate warmed, a greater range of plants prospered, each year partially decaying. Eventually the lakes filled with peat, becoming fens. The surface plants now had only rainwater to sustain them. Sphagnum mosses and bog cotton thrived, other plant life did not.

Sphagnum moss is curious stuff. It can hold up to twenty times its own weight of water in its pores and cells. In the bog it draws up and holds water as it grows, and as it decays and accumulates over thousands of years, it forms layer upon layer of peat. It is this process that forms the very deep bogs we have in Ireland. These raised bogs get their name from the fact that they are (or were) raised several metres above the surrounding landscape. A raised bog has a dome-shaped surface, and in some areas can be as deep as 13 metres.

From the Grand Canal you can see miles and miles of the worked bogs that provide fuel for power stations run by Bord na Móna, the company that harvests the peat. Toy-like trains transport the peat along narrow-gauge railways throughout the bog, occasionally crossing the Grand Canal, sometimes on movable and sometimes on fixed bridges. The bog has secrets. Every so often headlines are made when a human body or old bit of road is discovered preserved in the acidic, oxygen-deficient peat. So far around 1,600 artefacts have been discovered in Ireland's bogs, many of them giving valuable information about early communities. One such settlement was uncovered at Clonfinlough in Co. Offaly. The two broken paddles discovered there show a level of sophistication in the transportation of water not previously recognised. Another discovery was a single-plank walkway from Curraghmore townland, Blackwater. This dates from around 1550 BC, and was originally over 1 km long.

Even well-preserved butter has been unearthed. Not from 1550 BC though.

It's an interesting place, the bog, but it's fast disappearing, endangered not only by removal of peat for heating and horticulture, but by the changing climate. Less rainfall means the bog dries out. The bog fires we were seeing were the result of weeks of dry weather. Fire brigades were unable to contain the blaze for at least twenty-four hours. Huge areas of peatland were blackened. It was shocking to see. Gorse turned to charcoal, its yellow almond-smelling flowers extinguished. Trees with their fresh new leaves black and brittle. No birdsong. We crept between the banks in silence, our nostrils filled with the smell of smoke and barbecue. No guilty thrill now. I wondered whether worms and other underground creatures survived fires like this.

Just beyond Daingean we passed a stretch of towpath marked in the *Grand Canal Guide* as 'the red girls'. In the days when canal boats carried goods on the Dublin to Limerick run, there was a small house here where the daughters all had red hair. They were a favourite among the passing boatmen. After 'the red girls' came our first Bord na Móna lifting bridge. It was apparently open, but leaned at an alarming angle across the water. Surely we wouldn't fit beneath. I breathed in and ducked my head as we went under to help *Winter Solstice* through, praying the bridge mechanism would hold. I'm not fond of lifting bridges. I can never pass without imagining the span collapsing to push us down and trap us underwater.

On another trip the following year, we came to this bridge in late afternoon. It's a lonesome section of canal when you're on your own – black flatness stretches away. Silence. Dunes of milled peat. The bridge was closed as we approached. I expected it to rise at any moment, but it didn't. We tied *Winter Solstice* to a couple of trees, ropes trailing across the towpath, and went to see if there was anyone about. The small hut was empty. Nobody answered the phone number advertised in its window. We walked to the bridge and saw that it had a control panel with a pad of numbers, but had no idea of the code. Thoughts of pints in a congenial pub began to fade.

Another boat pulled up, a surprise on this less than busy waterway. We were delighted to have the company, and even more delighted to discover the skipper was someone with local knowledge. He had a story about this happening before. He knew the code for the bridge. We punched it in and watched the over-water railway rise. I have the code written in my *Grand Canal Guide*; I hope they don't change it.

The flotilla spent Easter Sunday night in Edenderry Harbour, reached by a 1 km cut off the main line of the canal. Sunshine had been replaced by low clouds, and on Easter Monday we woke to rain, not a bad thing in terms of quenching bog fires, but low skies and drizzle are dreary in the black, peaty flatness of the Midlands. Another end-of-holiday cloud draped itself over the boats as we set out for Lowtown, our destination in Co. Kildare.

Lowtown was another Shannon Harbour – full of boats for sale, 'projects' with optimistic owners, live-aboards and wrecks. There was also a chandlery and a few CCTV cameras, so it was considered a safe place to leave a boat. We planned to moor *Winter Solstice* there for a week, returning the following weekend. There's a canal junction at Lowtown. Go straight on and you eventually arrive in Dublin. Go right and you are onto the Barrow Line, a canal that goes to Athy in Co. Kildare, more or less following the route of the River Barrow. This was to be our next adventure.

We had company – Brian, who had organised the original trip, and his wife Anne were bringing their cruiser *Carian* to a boat festival in Athy, so we joined them. My parents came too, on board for daytime cruises and staying in bed and breakfast accommodation at night. That weekend we planned to go as far as Monasterevin in Co. Kildare, named after the monastery founded in the sixth century by Saint Evin of Cashel. It was, at that pre-bypass time, cut through by the N7, the main route from Dublin to Limerick. We'd travelled this road many times on our way to and from the capital, and thought of it as a gloomy place, grey with perpetual traffic jams, but we discovered a different Monasterevin when we pulled into Bell Harbour on Sunday afternoon.

Monasterevin had been constructed by the earls of Drogheda as an estate village. Their country seat was Moore Abbey, built in the seventeenth century, and they were responsible for the row of fine Georgian houses on what is now West End. The houses open straight onto the pavement, but across the road are gardens that go down to the River Barrow. Moore Abbey is possibly better known for the fact that Irish tenor John McCormack leased it from Lord Drogheda in 1924 and lived there, on and off, for twelve years or so.

McCormack wasn't the only artist the village had attracted: in the 1880s Victorian poet Gerard Manley Hopkins visited Monasterevin regularly during the five-and-a-half years he spent teaching at the Catholic University on St Stephen's Green in Dublin. It was something of a haven for a man who struggled with many demons. Hopkins converted to Catholicism in 1866, being received into the church by John Henry Newman, Cardinal and founder of the Catholic University of Ireland, which later became University College, Dublin (UCD). Hopkins was deeply torn between his vocations as priest and poet – he felt that religious inspiration was superior to artistic inspiration, and wherever they were at odds it was the poetic expression that had to be sacrificed. He experienced terrible conflicts between his love of and desire to write about the natural world, and his belief that this natural beauty must be denied, that higher religious experience must be all.

This struggle culminated in 1868, after Hopkins had written his purely ascetic poem 'The Habit of Perfection', in his burning all his poems. This seemed to have been a reaction to his reading of a biblical interpretation of Savonarola, fifteenth-century Dominican friar, orator and preacher of the brimstone school, specialist in prophecies of doom and eventual martyr. It was Savonarola who famously made a bonfire of the vanities in the Florence carnival of 1497, among which were books and artworks he considered to be profane.

Hopkins said he 'felt better for the delicious bog air of Monasterevin,' and we too came to appreciate it as a place of tranquillity, not traffic. Three bays of the old Bell Harbour, built for commercial canal boats, had been recently excavated, forming watery courtyards for the new warehouse-like apartment buildings, many of which were yet to be occupied. Advertising information showed a little boat with sails up, jauntily (and improbably) tacking along the canal. The same brochure referred to this simple harbour as a marina, but then advertisers always did inhabit a parallel universe. A couple of the new residents were taken in by it, shocked at the succession of real and not always glamorous boating neighbours, obliging them to hang net curtains. This gated community was a novelty – the building boom that would line the north Shannon with blocks of flats and semi-detached estates was just beginning. It was also a fine place to leave the boats for a week.

Monasterevin is a village full of bridges. We set out the following Friday evening, in convoy once again with our boating companions, immediately passing under a small lifting bridge (oh no!) that had to be raised for us by the lock-keeper. Beyond the bridge was an aqueduct, carrying the canal over the River Barrow and providing first-class views of the

Georgian houses facing the river. To our right, the railway bridge thrummed with Dublin trains. On the far side of the aqueduct, a branch line split from the main canal, passing under another bridge to the now derelict Mountmellick Line. Next was the humpbacked Moore's Bridge curving above the twenty-fifth lock and, finally, on our way out of Monasterevin, concrete darkness under the N7.

In the Patrick Kavanagh poem 'Lines Written on a Seat on the Grand Canal, Dublin', Athy appears as a place both distant and exotic:

> Fantastic light looks through the eyes of bridges
> And look! a barge comes bringing from Athy
> And other far-flung towns mythologies.

When Kavanagh wrote this poem in the late 1950s, canal boats still carried goods up and down the country, though they were no longer towed by the horses that would have to cross the river in Athy, pulling boats from river trackway to canal towpath. Passage for these horses was via the eponymous Horse Bridge that spans the river next to the deep lock that drops boats straight into the fast current. It could also take boat crew – handy, as there was no jetty below the lock for them to get back on board. *Carian* and *Winter Solstice* went into the lock together, our crews working the sluices from above. I was edgy. We would hit the river at right angles, its fast current tipping the flow over an open weir to our right.

All the way down in the lock I imagined a loss of power or my own incompetence causing me to be scooped sideways over the weir. As the lock gates opened, I kept my eyes straight ahead, put both engines hard forward and shot across to the other side of the river, turned left under the navigation arch of the bridge and slowed, remembering to breathe again. On the river bank ahead, within the town itself, I saw a line of boats, sunlight flickering on bunting and flags.

Athy was an ancient river crossing that became a garrison town on the edge of the English Pale. Like many border towns, it has a grisly history of burning and plundering. The name goes back to the second century and the inevitable river-crossing battle. Even before the Anglo-Norman invasions of the twelfth century there were regular skirmishes between Irish clans. This particular skirmish was between the Leinster men and the Munster men, and a high-born fellow called Ae was killed at the ford, so giving his name to the area – Ath Ae, the ford of Ae.

In 1417, Sir John Talbot, Henry V's lieutenant in Ireland, built a fine castle at the bridge to protect the inhabitants of the Pale and keep marauders out. Whites Castle is still there, and in fine condition as it's a private residence. I imagine there are ghosts aplenty, but the public are not allowed in to find out.

We tied our boats against the bank along with all the others, but weren't allowed to rest for long. Just upriver from the Horse Bridge, in to the right, a mighty hole had been excavated and filled with water, then attached to the river by a short channel. There was a new humpback bridge, constructed to take the trackway over this channel (on the Barrow, unlike on the canal, you never refer to the towpath as the towpath). The hole had been given the ambitious name of a marina, and it was to be opened this weekend by a couple of bigwigs. They needed boats to go into it for the photo opportunity and the 'blessing' of the new harbour. The thing was unfinished, and there were no jetties, not even a solid shore, just peaty mud you sank into, and that came into the boat on shoes and paws.

In order to get into the hole, boats had to pass under the new bridge. It was narrow and built of very unforgiving stone. We did this manoeuvre one at a time, each of us going downstream, then turning upriver to gain more control of the boat before having a stab at getting through the bridge. Our go, and downriver we went, then up, opposite the bridge, a turn across the current. The river caught us in our vulnerable beam-on position and whooshed us back downriver. Another go, another failure. The problem was that I needed to aim for my goal at speed, but I was afraid of hitting *Winter Solstice* off the corner. And they expected boats to regularly come in and out of here. Third time lucky? No. Fourth? The crew was getting tetchy and impatient, so there came a 'fuckit' moment, hard forward with the throttle, and in we went to the calm waters beyond. A small cheer went up.

The digging of the hole occurred at the start of the Celtic Tiger years, an intimation of things to come. A few years later the hole was filled in. There were never enough boats in Athy to make it a viable proposition. Another intimation of things to come.

Chapter Seven

That summer, we decided to go north to Lough Erne with the HBA. Two days before we were due to set off, Joe did his back in again. It was the usual disc problem, and we were dismayed. A visit from the physio was not encouraging – avoid sitting down, no bending or lifting, care getting into and out of bed. How could he even get to the boat when sitting in a car was so painful? Once on the boat, he would be of no use at all.

'You know,' said Joe after a day of gloom. 'Being on the boat might be a good thing. We stand in the cock-pit a lot anyway. And I can stretch out in the saloon for a rest.' I brightened for a moment, then tried to be sensible.

'How would we get you there? And you won't be able to do the ropes.'

'The car seat goes almost flat. And I could learn to drive the boat properly.' There was a short silence. The former seemed entirely feasible, but I wasn't sure I wanted to relinquish my superiority at the helm. What if he became more competent than me? Or wanted to do it *all the time*. And how would I manage the ropes? I wasn't able to do heavy, physical things. Although, thinking about it, there was nothing heavy involved, and since learning the trick taught to us by Mark Maguire nobody had to jump off the height of the bow to the jetty. Instead, the crew stood on the foredeck, rope looped in both hands, the middle section ready to throw. When the boat was close enough, you tossed the entire middle section beyond the cleat, then gathered it in.

I was still thinking up problems. Would I be able to pack the car and do all that driving? We could end up with two crocked people and two lively, under-exercised dogs on a boat far from home. But the alternative was no cruise to the Erne.

Winter Solstice was twenty-five minutes away at Angus Leavie's in Williamstown. I packed most things the day before while Joe lay on his back getting crabby. Departure day, and the first trip when I brought down pillows and duvet, books and food things that didn't need keeping cold. I shuttled between car and house with many small, lightweight loads. Once in Williamstown, I moved the boat to the corner that gave easiest access, carried the many small, lightweight loads aboard then went home for the second batch.

Joe was up and waiting. I lowered the car seat as far as it would go, stowed the remaining luggage in the boot and roared at the dogs, who were arguing in the back. Joe hobbled out and creaked into the passenger seat. Slowly, slowly, back to Williamstown. Easing a seized-up Joe out again was more difficult. A winch would have been handy, but eventually he was standing in the cockpit, shaken but ready to go. I, however, was not ready to relinquish the wheel just yet.

'It'll be tricky getting out of this corner,' I said. 'I'd better do it.' He gave me a look, but acquiesced, relieved, I think, at the reprieve. Anyway, we had help with the ropes from Angus and Noel, so were soon away into the expanse of the lake, up the river through Portumna Bridge and on to our first stop below the lock at Meelick, a test for our new regime.

It's not easy to keep your mouth shut when someone is learning to do a task you've already been doing for a year or so. It's even more difficult when that person struggles with the spatial world of left and right. Add to this an inexperienced rope person. I stood on the foredeck in exasperation as the bow swung out and the stern in, making it impossible for me to throw the loops of rope over the cleat. When the bow eventually came close enough, I missed. In the end, it was all my fault, apparently. In the lock itself, I zipped my lips.

We took it easy on our way to Leitrim, river we had cruised before, becoming familiar with each other's tasks while Joe's back steadily improved. Leitrim is a tiny place not far from Carrick-on-Shannon, and in those days it had a main street, a couple of pubs, a shop or two and a supermarket at the petrol station. It was a popular destination, and space for boats was limited. However, there was an alternative if you had stout shoes and didn't mind wading through mud and duck droppings. Just before the start of the Shannon-Erne

Waterway was a long bank where you could hammer in a couple of stakes and secure the boat. The walk to the village was messy if it had been raining, but no matter. You had a spot, the boat was safe and you could get to the pub. The HBA boats were already there. We put *Winter Solstice* outside one of the barges and went home for a few days.

The origins of the Shannon-Erne Waterway lay in a failure of a canal. The land between the Shannon and Erne is sprinkled with small lakes and rivers. One of these rivers, the Woodford, had already been made somewhat navigable at the end of the eighteenth century. In 1838, young engineer John McMahon was commissioned to survey a possible route that would join the Shannon to the Erne. Work began in 1846 on what was known as the Ballinamore-Ballyconnell Canal. His job was to link the small lakes and rivers with sections of canal, but by the time the project was finished fourteen years later amid spiralling costs it was already facing competition from the new railways. This, along with problems of draught (the canal in places was only three feet deep instead of the intended four-and-a-half feet) and maintenance, meant the canal's life was short – it was abandoned in 1869 after nine years and traffic of only eight boats.

In the later twentieth century as leisure boating became more popular various bodies began to lobby for the restoration of this canal and finally, in the late eighties, things began to happen. The International Fund for Ireland, created as part of the Anglo-Irish Agreement of 1986, targeted the restoration of this old waterway as a flagship project that would cement the new peace process, link the Republic and Northern Ireland and open up the neglected borderlands of Leitrim, Cavan and Fermanagh to tourism and economic regrowth.

It was not simple. Bridges had been built across the old canal that were too low to allow craft to pass underneath. Other bridges were broken. The canal itself had become a weed-choked drain. Locks had to be rebuilt in concrete, with the old cut stone used to face them to preserve the appearance. Banks and towpaths needed massive remedial work, as did the weirs.

The locks on this remade waterway were to be automated and operated using a push-button system, and bridges would be high enough to take the big cruisers becoming popular on the Shannon, boats that cannot navigate the Grand Canal. Crucially, hire boats would be encouraged to use the Navigation. A budget of €30 million was set aside, and in 1990 work began. Unlike the original canal, the project was completed on time and within budget. On 23 May 1994, it was opened to traffic with a ceremony at Corraquill Lock, near Teemore in Co. Fermanagh – the first lock on the system when travelling from the north.

The HBA boats were travelling up to the Erne in weekend stages, but weekends didn't suit us, so mostly we made our own way. Barges *en masse* move very slowly, so this was no bad thing. There are sixteen locks on the Shannon-Erne Waterway – eight going up to the summit and eight coming down again. It was a very different experience to the Grand Canal. They're big locks, somewhere between those on the Shannon and those on the Grand. We developed a system where I went in with *Winter Solstice* while Joe did things with the smart card out of sight above me. Loud buzzer noises advertised our progress. An initial hoot indicated the smart card had been accepted. Woo-woo-woo like a slow-motion police siren told us when the gates were opening or closing.

After the first eight locks, we passed under a high bridge into a roofless tunnel of rock, leading us to the highest point of the Navigation at Lough Scur – no soft mud, no forgiveness beneath the boat. As the rocky walls opened out, we appeared to have travelled through a time warp into a prehistoric land. Blackened stumps of dead trees poked shortened branches out of the water to either side as we followed the narrow, marked channel between them. A cormorant stood silent and black, drying its open wings on a lifeless branch. A dead stump of heron peered into the water's edge.

The chart showed standing stones and a dolmen close to the Navigation, along with Sheebeg Cairn, said to be the burial site of Finn McCool, the hunter-warrior giant of Irish legend who, enraged by the abuse thrown at him from the Scottish giant Fingal, began to hurl great lumps of land across the water to form a causeway so he could face down his abuser. These legends so often have a ring of the playground to them. Had his mammy never told him to ignore the taunts of uncivilised fellows like Fingal? It took a week to complete the causeway between Ireland and Scotland, by which time poor Finn was exhausted and not up to a fight with another giant, so he devised a Cunning Plan. He would put himself into a cradle and pretend to be an infant. We must assume he was able to hide the five o'clock shadow. When the frothing Fingal arrived, Finn's wife told him her husband was out, but look, she said, at my sweet babe asleep in the cradle. Isn't he a dote? By ye gods, said Fingal, if that's the child, what size is the father? I'd better get me back to my snug safe cave over in Scotland. Which is what he did, tearing up the causeway as he went.

Sheebeg Cairn stands atop one of the twin enchanted hills of Sheebeg and Sheemore, home of faeries and title of a slow air, popular with beginner musicians, by the blind harper Turlough O'Carolan. The atmosphere was such as we crossed the summit lake that I almost believed we would be captivated by the little people and lured away to be seen no more.

The navigation markers changed from those of the Shannon system (red on the left, black on the right when going upstream) to those of the Erne (red and white numbered semi-circles, pass on the white side). Down another eight locks with stops at Ballinamore and Garadice Lough, along the Woodford River and we were in Upper Lough Erne. The naming of Upper and Lower Lough Erne can be confusing – on the map the Upper Lough is lower (further south) than the Lower, the names being given according to which lake is further from the sea. It's also impossible to know while on the Woodford River whether you are in Fermanagh or Cavan, the Republic or Northern Ireland. The border runs up the middle of the river with the odd dip into Fermanagh, where the river is bypassed by the canal. We were unsure when to change our ensign.

The raising of the ensign is a funny business, but no joke if you are of a certain type, or are travelling in outland waters as opposed to the inland waters of a small island. The ensign is a flag proclaiming your nationality which the boat *wears* rather than flies. Some sticklers write letters to the boating press about improprieties in the wearing of an ensign. In Ireland, there seems to be little fuss about it unless you are in a military situation, but in Britain the rules are strict. Ministry of Defence legal obligations regarding the ensign give a maximum penalty of £1,000 for improper use. A permit is required, and the boat must be registered under the Merchant Shipping Act 1894. The ensign can only be put up if the owner of the permit is on board, and there are specific times when it should be worn: 15 February to 31 October, between 0800 and sunset or 2100, whichever is the earlier; 1 November to 14 February, between 09.00 and 18.00 or sunset, whichever is the earlier. I've heard that some people get out of their bunks at the crack of dawn especially to do this.

As members of the IWAI, most of the boats travelling north wore the club ensign. This is a blue flag, Tricolour in the top left corner, IWAI insignia on the bottom right. The difficulty was the Tricolour. There are some in Northern Ireland who would not take kindly to a boat on their territory with the flag of the Republic at the stern. There was even talk of stones having been thrown at boats displaying this flag. We were on Lough Erne partly at the invitation of the local branch of the IWAI and had no desire to offend anyone. So there was a compromise – an ensign designed for Lough Erne that was neutral. It had no national flag, or even the feeling of a national flag, but showed three horizontal bands of green (for the land), white (for the shore) and blue (for the water). In the end, we took down our Irish ensign before the Woodford River spat us out onto Upper Lough Erne and travelled naked until we reached our final stop on this journey at a new marina on Quivvy Water. This would be our base for the next few weeks.

Quivvy Marina is close to one end of the Ulster Canal, or would be if the canal had not been filled in, built over and generally abandoned. The HBA wanted to draw attention to its lamentable condition, and to a growing scheme to restore the canal, and so open up a route to Lough Neagh. The idea of the original Ulster Canal was to allow passage of goods from the ports of Belfast, Newry and Coleraine to Limerick and Waterford. A restored canal would be pleasure boats only.

The Ballinamore-Ballyconnell section of this through-route had already been surveyed by John McMahon in 1838. The blueprint for the Ulster Canal was in the hands of surveyor and engineer John Killaly. Killaly had worked on the Royal, an experience that appears to have given him preconceptions about canal construction. Three new navigations had been built in the north of Ireland – the Lagan, the Tyrone and the Newry, but Killaly's Ulster Canal locks were designed to be eighteen inches narrower than those on its sister navigations. What was he thinking? Cargo from Belfast and Newry would have to be unloaded from one boat and loaded onto a narrower vessel to travel along it.

You could say that the Ulster Canal was doomed from the start. Killaly recognised that the feeder supply of water from Quigg Lough near Monaghan was unlikely to be adequate to provide for the entire length of the canal. The lake needed to be dredged and made deeper, he said, but this never happened. The canal opened in 1841, but by the time the Ballinamore-Ballyconnell Navigation opened twenty years later, it had deteriorated badly and was largely unused. It closed for major repair work, but by the time it opened again, the Ballinamore-Ballyconnell Navigation was practically derelict.

However, here we were in 2003 having travelled along the restored waterway of the Ballinamore-Ballyconnell Navigation. The country appeared to be awash with money. The Shannon-Erne Waterway had brought such benefits to the regions it passed through: wouldn't it be glorious to do the same for the border counties between Lough Neagh and Lough Erne by restoring the forty-six miles and twenty-six locks of the Ulster Canal? The HBA intended to raise the profile of this project.

To get to the start of the Ulster Canal, you have to travel a little way down the Finn River to Derrykerrib.

The Finn was supposed to be navigable as far as Wattle Bridge, although not officially so, and we were going there for a photo opportunity. We set off in a convoy of various craft for our date with journalists and, we hoped, television cameras. The boats were got up in their best flags and bunting. We hitched a ride on one of the barges, and were on deck as two men came running down a field to the river's edge waving and shouting. Or at least their mouths were moving; we could hear nothing over the sound of the engine. As we came closer, we gathered that their agitation was in seeing such a fleet of boats heading for a drain.

'No way through!' they cried. 'Turn back!'

It's not easy to have a conversation from the deck of a moving boat in the middle of a river, but we did our best to reassure them that we knew what we were doing. They didn't look convinced, but on we went. Nobody went aground. Barges to the fore, we assembled at the bridge to find journalists and cameras waiting for us. The gathering of boats made it onto the evening news – it was August after all, the month for UFOs and lake monster sightings.

A week later, and we were chasing the HBA boats again. They'd gone to Belleek on the Fermanagh-Donegal border at the limit of the Erne Navigation after a stop in Enniskillen to show themselves off and attract attention to the waterways, but we'd been playing tunes at the Feakle Festival back home in Co. Clare. It's a long way from Quivvy to Belleek when seven knots is pretty much your top speed, and we had to negotiate the intricacies of Upper Lough Erne. It's a maze of channels and islands, with inlets masquerading as deep water waiting to capture you in their shallows. I was at the helm with the binoculars trying to make out the numbers on distant markers.

'Is that 33J or 33H?' I passed the binoculars to Joe.

'32D.'

'32D? Shit. How can it be 32D?' It was that per-spective thing again. The chart was small and flat. The lake was open and filled with obstacles.

After two hours of almost getting lost, it was a relief to see on the chart that the lake was about to split into two narrow channels that would weave and divide and finally join into one just before Enniskillen. It looked shorter to go via Carrybridge past the island of Belle Isle, a place that has been inhabited since the eleventh century. The earliest inhabitants were the MacManus clan – in those days the island was called, imaginatively, Ballymacmanus – and they were a scholarly lot. Cathal Óg MacManus, cleric, chieftain and scholar, who died in 1498, was one of the compilers of the *Annals of Ulster*, a chronicle of Irish affairs that spanned the years between 431 and 1540.

By the early eighteenth century, Belle Isle had become a major estate owned by the Gore family. Sir Ralph Gore built a house and created a garden that dipped its toes in the lake, but in 1830 the property was sold to the Reverend John Porter from England. It was the Porter family who built Belle Isle into the place it is today, extending the house and adding a tower. The Reverend's son, John Grey Porter, put the steamships

SS Belturbet and *SS Knockninny Rock* onto the lake. These boats ran a regular public service between Kilconny Quay in Belturbet and Knockninny, where he'd built a hotel, and on to Enniskillen.

Today, the house is owned by the Duke of Abercorn and is called a castle – amazing what a tower can do for a place – and you can rent it out for up to four-teen people if you're feeling particularly celebratory and flush. There's also a cookery school where you can do an intensive four-week course and gain a diploma, or, if you're corporate, it will give you a day of team building – preferable, I would think, to panting round a forest firing paint balls at each other.

The river wound its way through Carrybridge and on into Enniskillen. We kept going along Broad Meadow, past the castle, under two road bridges, past the Round O park and jetty and through a lock beside Portora Barrage, which is only closed when water levels are very low. Then we were out into the broad lough, the local name for Lower Lough Erne, with its increasingly rugged landscape of rising hills and wooded islands. The first part of the lower lake is as sheltered as the upper, but there's a line beyond which the chart warns you to beware of high winds and open water. The islands thinned as the channel wid-ened and, quite suddenly, there it was. A very broad lough. No wind to ruffle our composure. Just the very high Cliffs of Magho to our south as we chugged west, making us feel very small with no sheltered ref-uge in sight. We were glad to enter the slender River Erne that would bring us into Belleek.

The harbour was full – an unusual experience for it. Belleek felt isolated, a long way from the comfort of the islands and harbours closer to Enniskillen. You could get stranded for days if the wind got up, and it was very much a border town, not always a comfortable place in the time of the troubles. We had a spy helicopter hovering above us for most of our time there, joked about but not a joke. Not sure what it made of the jolly japes that happened on the day after our arrival.

Around mid-morning, people began to appear dressed as pirates. I was amazed at the outfits produced – not the ready-mades you hired from fancy-dress shops, but home-made confections. There were a couple of blokes dressed up as women (aren't there always?) with vast mono-bosoms squashed into bodices. There were, as you would expect, eye-patches and pretend parrots, but no authentic wooden legs. Not practical to have to hop along a narrow deck.

Joe and I lurked on deck smiling uncomfortably, partly because of the water-pistols. The pirates had them, and so did all the teenagers. There was a marauding cruiser complete with false cannons and pirate crew, whose role was to attack another boat and steal a Guinness barrel amid feeble bangs and plumes of smoke. The water-pistol thing got out of hand when a bunch of lads aimed their full load at a food-laden table on the poop deck of a boat two down from us. Dinner was destroyed. The mammy was not amused. I knew it would all end in tears.

That evening, while walking into town in search of food, a helicopter dropped onto a patch of bare land. Three squaddies leapt out with sub-machine-guns and ran down the street, turning from side to side. We laughed nervously as they flushed a tractor out of a side street.

From fake battles to real battles: back across the expanse of Lower Lough Erne to the Second World War military base at Castle Archdale, now a holiday centre with static caravans and campsites, but still surrounded by the old military infrastructure. Castle Archdale was the base for Catalinas and Sunderlands, the RAF flying boats that patrolled the North Atlantic searching for German U-boats. In the early days of the war, pilots had to navigate north and then go west, forbidden to fly over the neutral airspace of the Irish Free State. They could give some protection to the shipping convoys coming to the UK from Canada and the USA, but there was a defence gap in the mid-Atlantic that gave the U-boats free rein to do their worst. Hundreds of Allied merchant ships carrying essential supplies were being lost to the U-boats.

Huge pressure was put on Éamon de Valera and his Government by both the British and the Americans to allow British military aircraft to pass through Irish airspace, and eventually a secret agreement between de Valera and Sir John Maffey, Britain's representative to Ireland, brought into being the Donegal Corridor, a strip of Irish airspace between Lough Erne and the Atlantic. Catalinas and Sunderlands changed their course, and possibly the course of the War. It was a Catalina that spotted the *Bismarck*, the formidable German battleship.

On 18 May 1941, the *Bismarck* had left its berth in Gotenhafen (now Gdynia) along with a fleet including the heavy cruiser *Prince Eugen* and three destroyers. Their mission was known as Operation *Rheinübung,* and they aimed to prevent essential supplies getting to Britain by sinking the merchant ship convoys coming in from North America. The *Bismarck* and *Prince Eugen* hoped to reach the Atlantic without being spotted by the British. They headed north through the Kattegat between Sweden and Denmark. Their hopes to pass undetected were frustrated: they were spotted both by members of the Norwegian resistance and the Swedish cruiser *Gotland.*

The weather intervened, thick fog allowing the German ships to travel undetected to the ice-edged Denmark Strait between Iceland and Greenland. The British battle cruiser *Hood* and the battleship *Prince of Wales* caught up with them, the guns were out and the Battle of the Denmark Strait began. It was short and sharp, lasting just over fifteen minutes, but resulted in the sinking of *Hood* with the loss of all but three of its crew of 1,418 men. The British were hugely indignant at the sinking of *Hood*, one of their finest battleships, and wanted revenge. The chase was on to find and sink *Bismarck*, but she disappeared under darkness, and on 26 May she was well on the way to port in France, receiving congratulations for sinking *Hood.*

Two Catalina flying boats took off from Castle Archdale to continue the search. At the controls of one was copilot Leonard 'Tuck' Smith from Higginsville, Missouri, on loan to the British to oversee the pilots

Towed In A Hole in her berth near Killaloe with her proud new skipper.

A first view of Rampart 32 *Burma Star* in Poole, Dorset before she became *Winter Solstice*.

Rocking at Rockingham – barbecue at Lough Key Forest Park
with *Winter Solstice* in the background.

Winter Solstice wears the Lough Erne ensign, dinghy towed
behind. But the ensign is the wrong way up.

Approaching O'Connell Bridge on the River Liffey.

Winter Solstice coming out of the 3rd lock on the Circular Line, Grand Canal, Dublin. Huband Bridge is in the background.

Going down 21 metres in the first chamber at the Ardnacrusha
hydroelectric power plant.

St Mullins – the tide has turned, the aground boat is nearly afloat and Victor's catamaran is on its way.

Resting against the wall in Inistioge after the tide has gone out – let work on the hull commence.

Creating my own shade at Meelick Lock.

Boats settle into the mud berth in Waterford during the
Tall Ships Race, 2005.

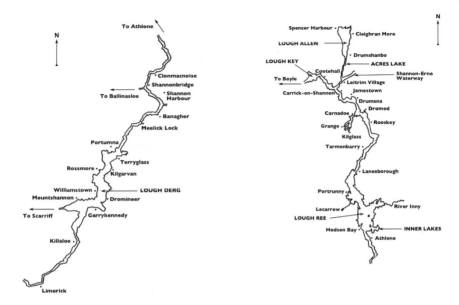

Map 1 The Lower Shannon: Limerick to Athlone
Map 2 The Upper Shannon: Athlone to Lough Allen

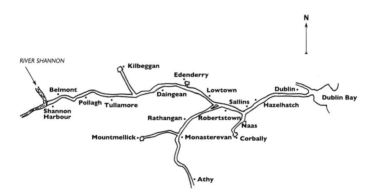

Map 3 The Grand Canal: Shannon Harbour to Dublin,
Lowtown to Athy

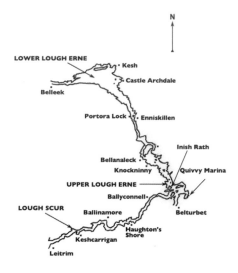

Map 4 The Shannon-Erne Waterway and Lough Erne:
Leitrim Village to Belleek

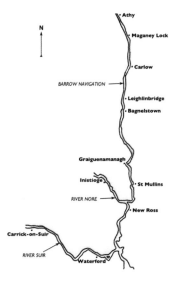

Map 5 The Rivers Barrow, Nore and Suir: Athy to Waterford,
Carrick-on-Suir and Inistioge

who would be flying the US-made Catalinas. He wasn't supposed to be there at all: the USA were yet to officially enter the war. It was Smith's Catalina that spotted the *Bismarck*. An aerial attack was launched from the *Ark Royal*, and at 10.30 a.m. *Bismarck* capsized and sank.

Concrete holding pens, the original docks for the flying boats, poked into the lake from the unfashionable side of the holiday centre, and this was where we found the barges. We tied *Winter Solstice* to the outer edge of one of them, and went exploring. There were miles of walks winding through woodland, edging the lake where the dogs galumphed and swam in the shallows. Every so often we came upon unexplained concrete aprons, or missile silos hidden among trees. A melancholic feel of abandonment mingled with holiday camp – there were caravans, barbecue and play areas, restaurant, bar and launderette, bicycles and water sports and many, many children.

The original big house still stood, along with a huge courtyard bordered by converted stables and outbuildings, one of which contained a museum. The most interesting items to me, and the most poignant, were the personal – letters home from servicemen, photographs, gas masks and ration books. Lives of the men who flew Sunderlands and Catalinas into the Atlantic became real.

On Upper Lough Erne is Inish Rath, a small island owned by the Hare Krishna Community. Our friends

Brian and Anne on cruiser *Carian*, also staying in Quivvy, told us that although the Community didn't particularly advertise the fact, you could turn up in your boat and visit the temple and, rather more temptingly, the vegetarian café, which had a reputation for top-class food. We decided we would have a jaunt. Other marina inhabitants, Jonathan and wife Daphne on vintage timber boat *Seagull*, decided to come too.

We set off into a clear blue day for the easy run to the island. As we drew close, I could see the length of timber jetty with fingers designed, really, for small, open craft. A plan was shouted between boats, and *Carian* made the first run in. Successful. We followed next on *Winter Solstice*, with *Seagull* coming in last. Half of each boat was poking out well beyond the short jetty fingers, but we managed to secure ourselves. We had the advantage of little wind, so there was hardly a pull on the lines. As we finished adjusting our ropes, a Hare Krishna monk appeared out of the trees – had they hidden cameras, we wondered, or divine knowledge? The latter idea was most appealing, but sadly not the case. He'd heard the boats and voices that carried easily from the shore to the buildings at the top of the island.

The shaven-headed monk led us up a track through trees to an elevated clearing on the twenty-two-acre island. I wondered what to expect. Brian had heard that we'd probably have to attend a talk of some kind in exchange for being allowed to look round and eat their food. The monk led us into the building next to the temple, and told us that someone would be there to see to us in a few minutes. It was disorientating to see the Krishnas on this island in Lough Erne instead of winding through English streets, a train of saffron-robed westerners with shaved heads and the occasional drum chanting:

Hare Krishna Hare Krishna
Krishna Krishna Hare Hare
Hare Rama Hare Rama
Rama Rama Hare Hare

In England, I knew them for their ascetic lifestyle and soup-kitchens, presuming they were part of a cult that attracted the vulnerable and lonely, but in India they are very much mainstream – Krishna is one of the myriad Hindu gods. In Bangalore, Karnataka, we visited their main temple set on a hilltop, vast and newly built with thousands of Krishna devotees queuing to visit every day.

A monk arrived to bring us into the rather more modest temple on Inish Rath, but with no promise of lunch. They were at the end of a celebratory weekend, and everyone was exhausted. The kitchens were closed. In the temple – a long hall converted for its purpose and filled with the colours of India – we were asked to sit, on the floor if we could manage it, and watch a video that would explain the Krishna lifestyle.

The members of this community, like those in monasteries everywhere, preferred an early rise. The day's spiritual work began at 4.30 a.m. (gulp) with sacred singing and chanting that continued for two hours. The next ceremony was at 7.00 a.m. (just time for breakfast in between?) and so it went on until the final event at 8.30 p.m. Our temple experience lasted for about an hour, then we had a cup of something hot and herbal and delicious in the garden. A wander about and back to the boats.

The Krishnas are deeply spiritual, but also keep a sharp eye on Mammon – how else would they raise the funds to purchase hills in Bangalore and keep communities going such as that on Lough Erne? Inish Rath is not only somewhere for devotees to spend time, it also offers Lake Isle Retreats. These programmes include yoga, meditation, eastern philosophy and vegetarian cookery. In Bangalore, after your spiritual freshening in the various temples on site, you are herded through the book store, encouraged to buy religious pictures and taken into a statue shop where they turn off the lights to reveal their luminosity. With so many versions of the same god, there's a lot of scope for shopping. It puts the icon shops in Ireland well into the shade.

Chapter Eight

*I*t was the two-hundredth anniversary of the Grand Canal, and the fiftieth of the IWAI. Emboldened by our canal virgins adventure, we decided to go by boat to Dublin, making the run into the city along with a few dozen others. Travelling in company was important – the canal in the city was a dumping ground for old mattresses, bicycles, fridges, cookers and, of course, shopping trolleys and traffic cones. We would have to contend with an overgrowth of weed clogging our engine intake and wrapping itself round the propellers, and there were gurriers – boats were a novelty on this section of canal, and gangs of small (and not so small) boys found them a great diversion. Other boaters had warned us to expect uninvited passengers as we sat trapped in a lock.

The journey to the Barrow junction was familiar territory, but this time we were on our own, not joining the rest of the flotilla until Hazlehatch on the outskirts of the city. An issue I'd been fretting about was how to manage the locks with only two of us. Going downhill was no problem, the water calm as the boat dropped quietly – a nudge forward and back with the engines was enough to keep *Winter Solstice* away from the walls and cill. But going up, with water pouring into the chamber through open sluices? We needed A Method.

Our canal virgins tutor came to the rescue with a comprehensive description of the stop rope system, and at lunchtime on the first day of our voyage we had the chance to try it out. Between one and two, all lock-keepers disappear for a lunch break, and you either have to wait or take yourself through. We didn't want to wait. The tailgates were already open, so I dropped Joe at the jetty below the lock and motored into the chamber, keeping to the left. While Joe closed the gates, I fixed a long rope to the cleat on the fore-deck and threw it (second time lucky) onto the top of the left-hand lock wall for Joe to pick up. He attached it to the bollard nearest the tailgate, almost level with the stern of *Winter Solstice*. Instead of switching off the engines, I put the port (left) engine gently forward while turning the wheel to starboard, away from the wall. This brought the stern in while the rope held the bow. We kept steady. In the days of commercial traffic, bargemen used this method, and you can still see marks on the lock chamber wall where decades of rope sawed into rock. The principle was that boat and line would work against each other, holding the boat close to the wall and preventing forward and aft movement.

Joe closed the tailgates, lowered the racks to close the sluices, then walked quickly to the breast gate footboard. Now for the test. Using our new lock key, Joe opened the port rack halfway, the initial surge of water keeping *Winter Solstice* against the wall instead of pushing her off. We began to go up. I could see Joe opening the rack some more and tensed, but we were OK. I began to relax. This was really working! He looked at me, and I gave him a thumbs up. He set the lock key to the second rack, opening the sluice, then moved to the other gate. Thumbs down. Enough for now.

Once I could see over the wall, and the water was settling, my confidence increased. Joe opened the other racks, and *Winter Solstice* swung violently across the chamber, hitting the wall on the other side. Even over the engines, I could hear Joe roar. I grappled with wheel and throttles, turning the boat this way and that as she lurched from left to right. I had no idea what was going on, but knew I was in big trouble.

At each of the next locks I was nervous, but we'd taken precautions, putting fenders at each corner to save the paintwork. We experimented with line length, making it successively shorter. Eventually we found our rope settling into the groove made by the old working boats and knew we had it right.

It was good to go straight on at Lowtown along the Dublin Line instead of turning right down the already travelled canal to Athy. We pushed on to Hazlehatch, going downhill now through six more locks, getting into commuter land, names familiar from AA Roadwatch traffic news, past Sallins and the turn onto the Naas Line. Finally we saw lines of boats ahead, and knew we'd reached Hazlehatch with its live-aboard boats, some with tiny garden plots and access to electricity. Both unfamiliar and familiar boats rafted out from the towpath – a holding pen for the trip ahead.

We'd travelled alone or in groups to this point, but from here on we would stick together. The starting point for the final haul into the city was to be the Twelfth Lock at the Lucan Road Bridge. This was both traditional and necessary. You needed two types of key to pass through the twelve locks into Ringsend – the normal lock key we carried with us and the one to open the padlocks. Waterways Ireland kept these locks locked to prevent unauthorised people (aka yobs, gurriers, bad lads, pranksters) letting water through and emptying the canal.

We left Hazlehatch that afternoon along with fifty or so other boats, aiming to spend the night at the Twelfth Lock and set off early next morning. Waterways Ireland had been cutting weed on the canal. There were great islands of it clumping across the water. You could almost walk across without getting your feet wet. The boat in front, a modern barge built in Holland, seemed to be going over the clumps without any trouble, so I did the same, as all good sheep do. Nothing much happened. The engine didn't overheat, and we moved along in a fairly straight line until we reached the jetty before the lock. I steered towards it, but somehow couldn't get close enough. There were two problems: the bank beside the jetty had a gradual incline instead of the sharp edge required to allow you to come alongside, and something was wrong with the boat. I was trying to go to starboard, but *Winter Solstice,* deeply unimpressed with all the weed I had steered her over, had other ideas.

'What are you doing?' shouted Joe, positioned with a rope at a bow that was not getting any closer to land.

'There's something wrong!'

'What's the matter? What are you doing?' Joe was getting louder.

'There's something wrong. She won't turn.'

'What are you doing? Turn her in!' Louder and louder. The problem on a boat like ours is that skipper can't hear crew and vice versa. Each blames the other for this.

Joe sprint-shuffled along the deck and leaned in.

'What's going on? Why won't you turn in. Jesus. You'll have to go back.'

'She won't fucking turn! There's something wrong!' I put her in reverse and had another go. We crabbed slightly closer to the jetty and stopped, partially aground. Joe flung the line from the bow and I did the same from the stern. We put out the boarding-plank and tottered across, then peered at the props.

There were plenty of helpers. The Dublin branch of the IWAI was out in force.

'Weed on the prop. You'll need the diver,' said Mick Kinahan.

'The diver?'

A local diving club had been engaged to keep the fleet mobile by removing detritus caught around shafts, props and rudders. As the Club wouldn't be out until the following day, we'd have to limp along. We pulled *Winter Solstice* through the lock with ropes; far easier than starting the engines and trying to steer her, settled next to another cruiser and walked back with the dogs to watch and add our muscle to the ever-increasing band at the lock.

There's something mesmerising about watching boats passing through locks. I like the rhythm of the process, cogs turning, sluices opening and always an edge of unease as boats sank into the dank depths. An under-construction barge owned by Becker siblings Mark and Cathy moved into the chamber. They'd bought the hull the year before, and had the metal superstructure built to their specifications. It was coming on well, but they were still in the camping stage. There was no glass in the windows, and steering seemed to be a complicated procedure involving cables, but she was on the water and her owners were immensely proud.

The old canal boats and the locks had a relationship with each other – the lock was the perfect size for the boat. This left very little room around the edges. The bow had to be pushed against the forward gates, which is what Mark did. We watched the barge steadily drop. It was a while before anyone noticed the flow of water pouring through gaps in the lock gate, then into the boat via glassless windows.

'Mister, Mister, can I get on your boat?'

We were in the lock and surrounded by small boys in various states of dishevelment.

'You can't, unless you have life-jackets,' we lied. 'Our insurance won't cover us.'

'Give us one of yours.'

'We don't have children's jackets. You can't come on.'

'Mister, Mister, can I get on your boat?' Sigh. Then someone told us to let a couple of them sit at the front. We put the binoculars out of sight away from possible light fingers, and picked three lads who were relatively polite.

'You can sit up there, but if anyone else gets on, you'll have to get off.'

'No problem, Mister.'

They were on the boat before we could say any more, jumping into the cockpit, peering into the saloon.

'Can we look inside? Can we?'

'Yeah, can we?'

'Please, Missus.'

'Well OK,' I said. 'Just a quick look.' Were there really only three of them? Seemed like six or seven.

'No you can't,' said Joe. Don't ever let them inside, our friend had advised. 'You go up the front or you get off.'

They perched on the coach-house roof on the foredeck, delighted with themselves, waving at their mates, twisting round to grin at us until we began to sink in the lock. Then they went very quiet, leaning their heads back to look at the oblong of sky above.

We stopped at the Strawberry Beds between Ballyfermot and Clondalkin. No strawberries there, just the old Guinness filter beds that used to supply soft water for brewing to St James' Gate Brewery, and Park West, a big new development of office blocks and apartments. We were astounded at the number and size of the buildings. The new M50 arced over the canal behind us, and the development raised its roofs to the heavens. Our boats raggle taggled along the bank, none of them the flashy modern 'gin palaces' increasingly seen on the Shannon. We were secure here – the public towpath ran along the other side of the water, so unless someone decided to swim, or possibly to lob projectiles, our boats would be safe while we celebrated the occasion at a reception with free food and wine upstairs in one of the tower blocks.

★★★

Our slot to catch the tide was just after 7 a.m. We moved slowly out of our berth in the inner Ringsend Basin, chugged through clear blue morning light to the outer basin and joined the queue of boats at the lock. We were quiet over cups of tea. The dogs, after a quick walk, had put themselves back to bed below. The larks among us were at the banter already, but I stuck to sipping my second cup of tea, taking in the morning, thinking of the journey ahead as we slipped into the sea lock along with two other small cruisers. The Dublin skyline was punctuated with cranes, some red, some green, already pecking away as Dublin's building boom built up momentum.

Out of the still waters of the canal basin and into the tide of the River Liffey, Dublin's artery. Turn right and we would pass beneath the East Link Bridge to the docks from where we'd sailed for England on many Irish Ferries ships, but we turned left, going upriver with the incoming tide. We paused at a jetty on the northside to wait until all boats were through the sea lock. The bridges ahead looked impossibly low.

We moved quietly up the river, tide just turned to carry us along, water low enough, in spite of my misgivings, to allow passage under the many bridges. The few people about stopped to stare, strolling with Sunday newspapers under their arms or hurrying as though to work. Were they dreaming? A flotilla of cruisers on the Liffey?

There were fifteen bridges before the end of Navigation at Islandbridge, some lower than others. With our mast down we had one of the smallest air draughts, but it was a close call for other boats on this rising tide. We had an estimate of how long it should take to reach our destination, but with all these boats on the move? The Liffey is lined with unforgiving walls, precious few places to tie up between bridges and no way of getting ashore unless you had sticky hands and feet.

We crept under the final bridge, Joe standing on the aft deck to check our clearance. Phew. We were through, up to the top of the Liffey, as far as anyone could go on a boat without lifting it. The end of the tidal section, where waters mixed with those from the Sally Gap near Kippure high in the Wicklow Mountains, 25 km of fresh water steadily picking up mud and peatiness and detritus on its way to Dublin, mixing with saltiness seeping up on the tide from who knew where.

Above Islandbridge was a weir and a world away from the city. The river's banks were verdant, free of the constraints of stone walls, and the water tranquil. We walked through trees to find members of the Dublin University Boat Club in a men's eight. Joe had memories of the place – his brother-in-law used to row for this ancient and venerable club. Its birth was announced in 1847 when the Pembroke Club amalgamated with the Dublin University Rowing Club, and it based itself at Ringsend, a stretch of water that was as rough and debris-ridden then as it is today. They stayed married until 1881, when one lot of members decided they could no longer abide the other – little changes in the affairs of humans. There was a schism, and the split-off club called itself Dublin University Boat Club in order to distinguish itself clearly from the Dublin University Rowing Club. Both did terribly well in regattas, including the prestigious Henley.

The move to Islandbridge came in 1898 at the same time as the re-marriage of the two club splinters, members presumably having forgotten (or at least forgiven) the cause of the split. They built a clubhouse and tidied up the river to make it more suitable for rowing. They continue to win prizes at Henley, and hold their own annual Trinity Regatta in the War Memorial Park at Islandbridge.

The tide turned. We followed our friends on Broom cruiser *Blackslee* downriver, ducking as we passed under the first return bridge. There were more people about this time to stare and wave and smile as we went by. I felt more relaxed too, as the tide was going out. At the end of the run of bridges, most boats turned right to wait for passage at the sea lock and rise into the outer basin at Ringsend, but we and a couple of other boats kept going. We wanted a taste of the salt, and not just the watered-down stuff in the river – the red-and-white bands of the Poolbeg chimneys beckoned. A ship stood at the dock to starboard. Maritime rules applied here and we were very small fry.

Our boats were following the route of the old Guinness barges, until 1961 an everyday sight on the Liffey. In 1873, Guinness built a new jetty at Victoria Quay to enable boats to load and unload at the brewery gates. The first boats to carry Guinness the mile from the brewery to Dublin Port were steam lighters, built for the purpose and named after the rivers of Ireland. There was *Lagan*, built by Harland and Wolfe in Belfast, then *Shannon*, a brute of a boat by all accounts, unable to turn in the river but with a rudder and propeller fore and aft so she didn't have to. Next came *Slaney, Lee, Boyne, Suir, Liffey, Foyle, Dodder, Tolka, Vartry* and *Moy*. Another, *Docena*, was brought over from England. The job of these lighters was to pick up the wooden casks at Victoria Quay and travel downstream with the tide to the Custom House at Dublin Port, where the casks would continue their journey across the Irish Sea on the waiting steamships. These barges and their skippers lived through dangerous times, continuing to deliver their wares even through sniping across the Liffey at the start of the Civil War during the occupation of the Four Courts.

There was another set of steam barges built for Guinness by Vickers at the Liffey Dockyard in 1927. This was a huge outlay for the company, which, with hindsight, was not a good move, but who could foresee the takeover of deliveries by the lorry? The new barges were busy until the mid-thirties and kept going, just about, until Midsummer's Day 1961, when *Castleknock*, on her final Liffey journey, travelled back from the Custom House with a load of empty barrels to her home jetty beside the brewery at St James's Gate.

We went further than the old Guinness barges, keeping out of the marked shipping lane – there was plenty of depth on the edges for a boat with a 2 ft 9 in draught. We kept a nervous watch all round. The further out, the smaller we felt. Past the containers waiting on the quay for delivery to somewhere, past the dirty end of the docks where tourists never go with its cranes and grubby warehouses. At Poolbeg Lighthouse, we stopped. Dollymount Strand stretched its gold around the bay. Ireland's Eye kept an eye. There was a bit of a chop to show us we really were at sea. The red-painted lighthouse, showing the way to the River Liffey since 1820, was far enough for today. We needed to get back to quieter inland waters while there was still enough depth to pass through the sea lock to Ringsend Basin. Beneath us, *Winter Solstice* gave a shiver and smiled a boaty smile, remembering her previous life as *Burma Star*, back in the salt of the English Channel.

We stayed in Dublin for a couple of weeks in the safety of Ringsend Basin with its new security gates, but then it was time to go back west. Once again we were in a flotilla, queuing at locks, but there seemed to be less urgency this time. The sun shone, people came out to look at the bunting-festooned vessels, have a chat or say how great it was to see so many boats. Old men talked of the days when canal boats carried goods along the Grand to the Shannon and on to Limerick. Our ears pricked up at this – we were heading that way ourselves, and into the Shannon Estuary beyond the City of Limerick.

It's no big deal for boats to cruise the coast and estuaries of Ireland – hundreds of people do it all the time. However, going into outland waters is an adventure for inland waters people in small, inland waters craft. A plan had been hatched earlier in the year for a small group of such boats to boldly go where only the intrepid had gone before, in large part due to the previous difficulties of getting through Limerick – only during a tiny time window (between twenty minutes and an hour) could you get under Baal's Bridge. There was either inadequate water draught, inadequate air draught or too strong a flow on the tidal river. You also had to contend with the Ardnacrusha hydroelectric plant.

This changed in 2001. Shannon Development, Waterways Ireland and Limerick Corporation were all eager to improve the navigation through Limerick, but it was the Corporation who came up with the clever idea. The city was to have a new main drainage scheme. Why not route one of the interceptor sewers down the Abbey River (the navigable river that bypasses River Shannon rapids) and through the tidal lock at Sarsfield Bridge? This new sewer could form the base of a weir, while gates on Sarsfield Lock would hold back enough water in the basin created by the weir, so giving a minimum depth whatever the tide. This came to pass, and, on 20 July 2001, Síle de Valera, then Minister for Arts, Heritage, Gaeltacht and the Islands, opened the new Limerick Marina amid great fanfare and fuss.

It was 7.30 in the morning when we set out from Kincora Marina in Killaloe. We were lucky in our 'late' start – the first batch of boats had left at 5.30. Once under the bridge at Killaloe, we were into new territory – the flooded area, a lake that had once been a valley with a river running through it, now providing the head water for the Ardnacrusha hydro-electric power station, opened in 1929. We'd been told to watch for chimneys poking out of the water – a good reason to stick to the marked navigation. It was a clear, calm morning, and in the distance we could see Parteen Villa Weir. To the left it resembled a bridge with half a dozen supporting pillars, while on the right it looked like a giant's garden wall. The boats ahead of us were on course for the giant's wall. A gap between two high pillars steadily came into focus, topped with a guillotine gate – and I'd been nervous passing under the Bord na Móna bridges on the canal.

Parteen Weir is the point where the Navigation leaves the Shannon. Up to this point, the river has meandered 185 km down country from the Cuilcagh Mountains with a fall of only 12 m. From Parteen, it drops 30 m in just 19 km, becoming a series of waterfalls and rapids. We followed Freeman cruiser *Lotus Two* through the gap in the wall while I thought of Marie Antoinette and French Revolution beheadings. We were being sent, along with most of the water from the Shannon, along a canal to the power station at Ardnacrusha, bypassing the Falls of Doonass below Castleconnell, a once-magnificent series of waterfalls now emasculated by the diversion of water to fulfil the electricity needs of Ireland. We cruised through O'Briensbridge, under the road bridge we'd driven over many times, and into the headrace of Ardnacrusha.

From the headrace, the buildings of the power plant look relatively insignificant, or at least fairly low to the water. We tied our boats to a short jetty at the lock entrance to wait our turn, then we were through another guillotine, sandwiched between *Lotus Two* and *Blackslee*. Beneath us was 21 m of water in a chamber made of rock. Behind us, held back only by the giant tailgate, was 185 km of Shannon. Down we went, hanging on to bars recessed into each green-slimed side wall with boat-hooks or gripping the rusty, slimy chains with grubby hands. I looked up to see a small bright rectangle of light and was glad we were not on our own. Finally, in front of us, a line of light appeared below the next guillotine gate and we cruised into the second lock chamber. This one was a mere 9 m.

Then we were released into the tailrace with its wild greenery and drooping trees, a canal blasted out of rock when Ardnacrusha was built and only seen by those on the water. We were met by Pat Lysaght in a small, open boat. Pat had lived on this part of the river all his life, and was to be our guide for this last section. The water was still, all quiet but for the chug of engines along the 2.4 km to the end of the tailrace, then under Parteen Bridge and back into the waters of the Shannon, for a short while at least. Finally we turned left into the Abbey River, a backwater avoiding the Curragour Falls on the Shannon. It was twisty, the river was tidal and I was thinking about the lack of air draught under Baal's Bridge. We came to a sharp right turn under the Abbey Bridge, the entrance to the disused Park Canal catching my eye on the bend. I put *Winter Solstice* hard to starboard, under the Abbey then almost immediately under Baal's Bridge, straight ahead past Barringtons Hospital, under Matthew Bridge, handbrake turn and we were into the new Limerick Marina behind the Hunt Museum.

It was entrancing being in the centre of Limerick on our boats, especially on a Monday morning. We attracted a lot of attention. A parade of faces showed itself at the windows of the tax office towering above, and there was a constant flow of visitors to the pontoons. The hot, sunny weather helped. A few dignitaries did their dignitary bit, a requirement for any boating occasion on the inland waterways. As evening fell, the tide went out and we stayed afloat in deep, untroubled water as the Shannon sucked itself back out to sea. The security gate closed for the night, access by smart card only. We settled in til morning.

The next day was overcast, but our spirits were not as we left our moorings in time to catch the outgoing tide, turning left into the refurbished Sarsfield Lock adjoining the Shannon Rowing Club building on Wellesley Pier, a man-made island. We had a brief stop in the Limerick Docks so people could take on fuel. Not brief enough though for us, itching as we were to get going, to leave the city behind, to get away from the rank smells, oversized tanks and disinterest in we pleasure boaters. This was a place for serious craft, not a frivolous crowd on a jaunt.

Then we were off, feeling at sea already with the change in markers to international maritime, red to starboard as we went downstream and green instead of Inland Waterways black to port. Fergal Kerney and his elderly father John led the way on *Tan Juan*. They had done this before in the difficult times before the new marina, a team who loved the challenge of a twenty-minute window to pass under a low bridge with plenty of tidal calculations. The sun came out as the boats strung along the river, the tide picking us up and speeding us on our way. There was no wind, a major relief until we hit the fog – still air leaves fog sitting instead of clearing. It thickened as we passed the Aughinish aluminium factory across the water from Shannon Airport. One minute we were watching an Aer Lingus flight taking off, the next we were peering ahead trying to see the boat in front. Today, boaters heading to the estuary go equipped with GPS and radar, but Joe and I didn't even have the paper chart. We were following our leader and had to keep in close, listening for information on the VHF radio.

As the fog finally lifted, a cry went up – dolphins alongside, smiley faces dipping in and out of the water, watching us watching them. We passed the Killimer-Tarbert ferry carrying cars and passengers between Clare and Kerry, arriving at Kilrush Marina, our destination, in time to catch the sea lock during its open-at-both-ends period. One by one, we slid into our pre-booked berths.

On the next day, a few of us took off on a day trip to Carrigaholt, further down the estuary. The weather was variable and threatening to turn stormy as we left Kilrush on the tide. Ahead of us, hanging beneath a cloud, was a waterspout. These curious phenomena occur most frequently over tropical or subtropical waters during the warm season. As we were none of these things, Ireland not having a warm season in the usual sense of the word, we were privileged to see this and also unnerved. Although a form of *weak* tornado, they can still cause problems for small craft caught in their vortex.

Waterspout is something of a misnomer, giving an impression of water being sucked into the cloud above. Looking at our waterspout, we could see that it didn't do that. It was an inverted cone hanging beneath a dark, fat cumulus cloud. In the centre of a waterspout is a low-pressure vortex surrounded by a rotating funnel of updraughts filled with condensed water vapour. This funnel seems to reach towards the water from the cloud. As it begins to form it causes disruption to the surface beneath, sometimes lifting the water for a metre or more.

In 1872, a waterspout caused great upset in Wanlockhead, the highest village in Scotland. It had been hot and airless for a few days, typical thunderstorm weather, and so it was no surprise when a black cloud was seen building over Stake Moss Hill. This was the place where witches had been burned at the stake, almost within living memory – two old women from the village were said to have been condemned as witches in the mid eighteenth century for practicing herbal medicine. Before they died, they told the other villagers, who were against their sentence, that they would return. So when there was a blast, a crash like thunder, then a strong gust of wind, followed by a waterspout, well, surely it was the mad incarnation of an enraged witch, twisting over the mountain top, then dropping as though to tap the mountain's shoulder before spiralling back into the dark cloud above.

Waterspouts have been blamed for those reports of raining fish and frogs loved by gossip-mongers and tabloid newspapers. Some of these accounts are simply bonkers, while others are wishful thinking: far more thrilling after stormy weather to believe a waterspout puked its live contents than to accept it was heavy rain flushing worms from their burrows and frogs from their pools.

However, there *are* descriptions that can be believed. In 1947, A.D. Bajkov, a biologist with the

Louisiana Department of Wildlife, experienced a fall of fish from the sky. He gave this report:

> There were spots on Main Street, in the vicinity of the bank, averaging one fish per square yard. Automobiles and trucks were running over them. Fish also fell on the roofs of houses … I personally collected from Main Street and several yards on Monroe Street, a large jar of perfect specimens and preserved them in Formalin, in order to distribute them among various museums.

In 2010, there was a fall of hundreds of spangled perch in Lajamanu, a small town in Australia. Christine Balmer was on her way home when the downpour began:

> These fish fell in their hundreds and hundreds all over the place. The locals were running around everywhere to pick them up …

Low tide in Carrigaholt and four of our boats, *Winter Solstice* included, rafted out at the bottom of a very high quay wall designed not for pleasure cruisers but for fishing vessels. A couple of others anchored off and came ashore in dinghies. We climbed the ladder, and walked to the village in search of a pub. We found one, full to the gunnels with holidaying families in discarded waterproofs eating and drinking, children full of fizzy drinks running amok. All you could do was join them.

It was late afternoon. We'd been loath to abandon the warmth of the pub, and had to hurry to catch the tide. The weather was closing in as we cast off, clouds building over the mountain ranges, then rolling in on top of the boats. We could hear thunder even over the sound of the engines. A small timber boat, out in the middle of the estuary in a thunder storm. It was suddenly important to go below and start the dinner. After all, it would be late enough when we reached harbour. I was very busy down there as electric forks from the dark, dark sky earthed themselves all around.

We stopped a night at Foynes on our way home and watched great ships come in on the tide, passing so close to our little pleasure jetty we could almost touch their rusting hulls. They were on their way to the deep water seaport beyond, the second biggest in the country. As we came on deck after dinner, the sky was streaked with the red of a breathtaking sunset show.

The history of Foynes was not only that of shipping. On 16 December 1935, *The Irish Times* announced that it was to become the European terminal for transatlantic flights to Botwood in Newfoundland. The craft that landed in Foynes were flying boats, and they changed the nature of world travel. I had never been clear about the difference between flying boats and seaplanes, and tended to use the two interchangeably. Seaplane was probably the favourite as it seemed more modern, a sea-going radio to the old-fashioned wireless. But I was wrong. The flying boat is, in fact, a type of seaplane, of which there are two main models

– the float plane and the flying boat. Float planes are the ones we see today occasionally landing on Lough Derg – the Cessna 172 is an example. The Cessna has two floats, a bit like surfboards, mounted underneath the fuselage on struts, that touch down on the water. The flying boat, however, is a much bigger affair, and the body of the craft lands in the water so it sits like a normal boat.

The Boeing 314 'Clipper' served transatlantic passengers flying from Foynes to Botwood. Pan American World Airways' *Yankee Clipper*, piloted by Captain Harold Gray, was the first to land at Foynes on 11 April 1939. The first mail flight followed on 28 June, with the first passenger flight landing two weeks later on 9 July – the beginning of the regular Pan Am service from New York to Southampton. A brave new world available only to the few – the cost of this inaugural flight was $675 return, around €5,000 in today's money.

For a few years, the tiny village of Foynes became the threshold of an exotic world touched by the rich and famous, including John F. Kennedy, Winston Churchill, Humphrey Bogart, Ernest Hemingway and Yehudi Menuhin. During the Second World War, it was one of the biggest civilian airports in Europe. Ireland was, of course, neutral throughout the war, and all flights in and out of the airport were civilian, not military. This did not mean, however, that military VIPs could not be transported. When the US entered the war in 1942, Foynes became an even busier place, and its neutral role was certainly in doubt (similar to

Shannon Airport during the Iraq war). Secrecy surrounded the flights. Military VIPs were forbidden to
wear their uniforms while on land at the terminal, but
on long bad-weather stopovers they were apparently a
common sight in the bars of Foynes and Adare. There
was an increase in flights when a new American car-
rier, American Export Airlines (AEA) joined the route.
They used the Vought-Sikorsky VS-44 flying boats
with a much longer range than the B314s, able to fly
directly from New York to Foynes.

One of the senior pilots with AEA was Captain
Charles Blair, who, in 1945, flew the last scheduled flight
from Foynes to New York. Blair was an all-American
hero, flying since his late teens, a wartime pilot who also
tested aircraft. His heroism and glamour quota increased
when he married the screen beauty Maureen O'Hara
in 1968. They met on a flight to Ireland.

The end of the war saw the end of Foynes. On 29
October 1945, Captain Wallace Cuthbertson piloted
Pacific Clipper on the final Pan Am flight from Foynes
to Lisbon. Business moved across the river to the new
transatlantic Shannon Airport, and on 24 October
the first flight from America to touch down on land
instead of water, a Pan Am DC-4, arrived in Co. Clare.

Our trip back to the inland waters had to be timed as
carefully as the trip out in order to get us all through
Ardnacrusha. We were in the tailrace, and seemed to
be barely moving. In fact, most of us were struggling
to make any way at all. *Winter Solstice*, even with her
two engines, was creeping. Halfway up the tailrace was

a small, recently installed jetty that one boat skipper had grabbed onto, the rest of us attaching ourselves like sticky flies.

The problem was that, unlike on our trip down, Ardnacrusha was running two of its turbines. There had been a good deal of rain, enough for the plant to make electricity. It is a curious fact that although boats were permitted to navigate through Ardnacrusha by arrangement, the lock-keeper was not allowed to tell boaters when he was about to turn on the turbines and so increase the flow of water through the tailrace and the Abbey River. In this age of compensation, it seems the ESB was afraid it would be held responsible for mishaps to boats if it told people what to expect. If it left them ignorant, however, and therefore more likely to suffer some kind of calamity, it would not be liable.

Late afternoon, and our plan was in disarray. We had two batches of boats to get through two very deep locks followed by a crossing of the flooded area to Killaloe. Travelling in the dark on a boat across an expanse with possible chimney hazards is not recommended. We were on the outside of the stuck-together flotilla, which was lucky for us – although allocated to the second batch, it would be too difficult to rearrange ourselves. We crept towards the lower lock.

The keeper raised us so very, very slowly, being considerate, but in reality making us want to put a firework under him. Each boat batch had someone with GPS and the relevant waymarks. It was almost dark when we reached Killaloe. It was completely dark when the second lot finally tied up for the night.

Chapter Nine

*W*e'd left *Winter Solstice*, along with the dozen or so other boats of the HBA, at Ardreigh Lock, the start of the Barrow Navigation. We were impatient to get going, to catch up with those who were already *en route*. It was approaching midday on Saturday as we stowed dogs and goods on board. I started the engines and Joe loosed our lines, Carlow in our sights.

On the previous weekend, we had lingered in Athy for the town's Festival, the first stage of the HBA cruise to Waterford for the start of the 2005 Tall Ships Race, the first time the race had set off from an Irish port and the cause of enormous excitement. Ardreigh is a couple of kilometres south of Athy as the water flows, a place, like many on the Barrow, of derelict mills – the last of these, Hannon's Mill, survived until the 1920s, and you can feel the ghosts on a still summer evening.

The river is bypassed at twenty-three points on the way south by weir and accompanying lock (hence its designation as a navigation) to allow boats to avoid the frequent shoals and rapids. It's an awkward river in some ways, shallow – sometimes too shallow – in a normal summer, and in winter roaring its way under many low bridges, carrying sand from one part and depositing it in a different, often more inconvenient spot, forming ridges and banks that change every year. Boats went aground on these unpredictable sandbanks. There were also difficulties for the crew – a dearth of jetties at the locks. We'd already experienced this coming from canal to river in Athy – sheer walls and nowhere at all for Joe to get back on board. He had to cross the Horse Bridge to the other side of the river where I could pick him up. The problem at Ardreigh was not walls, but a steep, nettled bank on the downstream side of the lock.

'You'll have to bring the bow right into the bank,' said Joe as *Winter Solstice*, the dogs and I steadily dropped in the lock. The bow on *Winter Solstice* was very high but there was little choice – no good putting the stern into the bank with the risk of the propeller hitting a rock or picking up branches and thick weed. I was expecting shouting, and indeed there was some, but on my part, not Joe's.

'Get on! Quickly! For God's sake! The stern's coming round!' Poor Joe. It wasn't easy, but finally he was aboard and we were away.

There were 20 km and three more locks before we reached Carlow and the other boats. Carlow is one of those towns that has turned its back on the river. We passed run-down warehouses and old mills with a sense of decay. Waiting to go under the bridge at Carlow were three or four cruisers, but we were relieved to see no barges. Graiguecullen Bridge, dating back to 1569, is the lowest bridge on the Barrow – indeed, on the whole of the inland waterways – and it was barges that were most likely to clip the low arch under the bridge with their substantial wheel-houses and broad beams. There are numerous, possibly apocryphal, stories of canal boats reducing their air draught by increasing their ballast with a classroom of children, but the schools were on holiday, and head teachers these days would perhaps be less accommodating.

An ancient wall rose from the waste ground beside our moored boats. There was an abandoned feeling about the ruin as I walked the dogs in its shadow that evening – hard to believe this was a Norman castle overlooking the river. All efforts to connect the town to the Barrow seemed to have been given to the other side just above the bridge in Graiguecullen, where a new Town Park opened in 2003. Next morning we took the dogs across there via the Millennium Footbridge for their constitutional, spending most of our time in the informal 'parkland' area. This is described by the architects as being:

> … configured as an informal walking and sitting area. A large earth configuration gives form and scale to the overall park. This moat or motte is configured as a counterpoint to Carlow Castle, echoing the defensive position which the park has on the river. It also symbolises the Norman history of Carlow in an abstracted manner.

Carlow seemed to be paying more attention to (and spending money on) an abstract version of the castle than the real thing.

Carlow Castle was built, first as a motte and bailey fortification, after the Norman invasion of Ireland to protect this important river crossing. An invasion that very possibly began with a woman – in 1152 Derval O'Rourke was abducted, along with her cattle, by Dermot MacMurrough, King of Leinster, when he raided the lands of Derval's husband Tiernan, holder of the northwestern kingdom of Breifne. Derval was returned a year later after who knows what humiliations, leaving the wounds of her taking festering in the family – if something as trivial as cutting down the wrong tree can, and does, cause a family feud for generations, then one can understand how wife-stealing would be grounds for wholesale invasion.

So although it is possibly fanciful to put what happened next down to a wifely abduction, fourteen years later Dermot, as recorded in the *Annals of the Four Masters*, was driven from Ireland by Derval O'Rourke's family. Dermot whispered in the ear of Henry II of England, who was ready to be whispered to – he was already considering the invasion of Ireland. He issued a writ giving permission to any of his men in any of his lands to aid Dermot. In late spring 1169, the Norman invasion of Ireland began with Dermot and his men joining the forces of Robert FitzStephen and Maurice de Prendergast, who had sailed from Milford Haven in Wales to land on the coast of Wexford.

The 'fixer' for Dermot was Richard FitzGilbert de Clare, also known as Strongbow, who should have become Earl of Pembroke after his father Gilbert. However, for reasons that are not altogether clear, Henry II refused to recognise Strongbow's rights to the lands and title. Richard was understandably peeved, and therefore very happy to listen to the plottings of Dermot. He was also offered the hand in marriage of Dermot's daughter Aoife, though what she thought of this arrangement we are not told. Strongbow would also inherit the kingdom of Leinster on Dermot's death – if only they could regain it.

Strongbow and Aoife were married in Waterford Cathedral in 1170, Dermot died the following year and Strongbow became King of Leinster. Over the following years loyalties between the Anglo-Norman invaders switched back and forth in a dizzyingly confusing manner, but during this time Hugh de Lacy, one of Henry's men, built the first castle at Carlow. The castle we see today was built circa 1212 by William Marshall. Having made his reputation as a knight in the Anglo-Norman court he married Isabel, daughter and heir of Strongbow and Aoife. He was forty-three, she seventeen. It was William, of course, who inherited the de Clare titles, not Isabel. She had the children – five girls and five boys – all of whom survived. They must have been tough stock.

Carlow was an excellent example of a Norman castle, and remained in reasonable condition until 1814, when a local physician, Dr Philip Parry Middleton, had the grim idea of fitting it out as a private lunatic asylum, no doubt to contain rather than treat its inmates. He took on the lease of the castle and went about its conversion with enthusiasm but little understanding of DIY. In 1904, Lord Walter Fitzgerald explained in a paper given during a tour of the castle and later published in the *Carlow Sentinel* that:

> Dr Middleton adopted what he thought was the speedier process of converting the vaulted interior into additional space by means of blasting powder. The result of his ignorance and folly was the collapse of the eastern half of the castle leaving it in the condition we now see.

We pulled in behind the other boats gathered at St Mullins, waiting for the tide and the final run to Waterford. St Mullins is a long way upriver from the estuary, at the very end of the tidal waters, and when the tide goes out it really does go out. Just below the lock in St Mullins is the Scar, and looking at it during low tide you wouldn't believe you could ever row a shallow skiff over it, never mind drive a cruiser. Fishermen were standing on rocks, up to their ankles in water. Children skittered stones to the other side of the river, perched in the middle without getting their feet wet. Boaters fretted about their water draught.

High tide was due in a couple of hours, so once we'd secured the boat we joined everyone else at the lock to check the water level beyond. There was a boat moored on the other side of the lock. Strange. According to our calculations there shouldn't have been enough water to float it. Then we noticed the angle. Listing badly, this boat was going nowhere. Sod's Law at play. Such a quiet place, normally, a place in which, having missed the tide, you could while away the morning without fuss or attention and sneak off when it rises again. Hardly to be expected, several boatloads of skippers and crew to watch your discomfort. The people on board were sanguine enough, although frustrated at the wait. A fifteen-minute delay in leaving had been enough to trap them there.

Our flotilla's departure was organised by water draught. Victor was first into the lock with his sailing catamaran and a draught of practically nothing. Behind him was an old Dutch canal boat, also with negligible draught. As Victor floated out of the lock, the aground boat came unaground and the first lockful was away. The rest of us were released one by one into the still-filling river and set off downstream on the just-turned tide.

Below St Mullins, the Barrow changed its nature, turning into a river from another, more exotic country, set in a deep gorge with layers of trees climbing high, steep sides. No houses, no road, just the river running between wooded walls. Alligator logs rested beneath trees at the edges, watching us with their wooden eyes. Herons stood rigid on stones in the shallows as we passed from heavy shade into sunlight and back as the river snaked. Coming out of the deepest section of the gorge, we turned back on ourselves in a hairpin bend, waving at the crew on the other side of the loop. A different, quieter world than the Shannon.

Just over 12 km downstream from St Mullins was Ferrymountgarrett Bridge, shortly followed by the inflow of the Nore, the second of the rivers known as the Three Sisters: the Nore, the Barrow and the Suir. As with the Shannon, legends surround the birth of these three rivers that give water to much of the South-East. From the English poet Edmund Spenser, writing his epic poem *The Faerie Queene* for Elizabeth I, we have the nymph Rheusa wandering happily about the Slieve Bloom Mountains when Blomius the Giant comes upon her. It is not a happy meeting, or at least not for the nymph:

> Under Slewbloome in shady grove was got,
> This Gyant found her and by force deflowr'd;

This unfortunate incident led, as nymph–giant couplings tend to do, to the birth of a geological feature, in this case the rivers Nore, Barrow and Suir. Spenser follows the classical tradition, referring to the rivers as 'three faire sons'. However, it is from Irish myth that the rivers became the Three Sisters – they are three of the seven secret streams of knowledge that flowed from Connla's Well, the source of all wisdom in ancient Ireland, the eruption of which gave birth to the Shannon when Sinann, lady of the *Tuatha Dé Danann,* tried to possess the Well's secret knowledge.

We were going as far as New Ross that day, and needed to complete this section of the journey on the outgoing tide – you could use up a lot of diesel trying to battle against the fierce tidal current. The trick was to leave St Mullins when the Scar was sufficiently covered, but not so soon that we arrived at Ferrymountgarrett Bridge before the river dropped enough to provide headroom for us to get under.

In New Ross, works had just finished on a float of new pontoons close to the town, and this was where we aimed to stop. What we hadn't realised, though, was that this just-built New Ross public marina was not yet attached to the shore. Dogs on board. Oh dear. And people needing supplies and pints. There were dinghies, of course, as transport, but our dogs, especially sheepdog Frankie, were not impressed with being manhandled from boat to dinghy. In the end, after much faffing and discussion it was decided that we would move to an old timber jetty a few hundred metres upstream. This was a jetty designed for shipping, not little inland waterways craft, and so when we pulled in we had to settle down by the supporting legs of the structure – still unable to get off. I don't think Joe and I made ourselves popular with our worries and fussing. They were just dogs after all. We might have decamped altogether and returned to St Mullins, but evening approached and we were not yet confident to travel this tidal water on our own in such circumstances.

One thing we did discover from this trip was that our hounds had very good holding tanks. They could go for hours without a toilet break if necessary, and were very patient of the whole business. It was Joe and I who were stressed. As usual, we were tied to a boat

tied to a boat tied to the jetty – for obvious reasons
it's not sensible to have a heavy steel canal boat on the
outside of vessels made from timber or plastic, so the
barges acted as jetties for the rest of us. Up we went
as the evening wore on. Somewhere around midnight,
we drew level with the shore. Tricky enough climbing
with dogs from stern to bow over railings and a rush-
ing ten-knot tide, but we made it.

The following day we left for the final push as the
tide turned, picking up speed as the river rushed out,
carried eventually under the high Barrow Bridge to
join the Suir at Cheekpoint. Here we turned right
upstream towards Waterford and our mud berth. Some
of us had been to look at this berth before, Joe and I
among them, taking photos at low tide, checking for
sharp debris in the mud that could cause problems
for a hull that sank onto it. For this is what the HBA
skippers planned to do – dry out twice a day with
the retreating tide to refloat as the water came back
in. Many relied on the knowledge of the trip organisers, trusting that all would be well, but none of us
had done this before. In our more delicate timber boat
we were in a fortunate position, as we would attach
ourselves to the outside of the flotilla where there was
always enough water to stay afloat even at low tide.

Nobody, however, was thinking about this on
Wednesday 6 July as we cruised along the shipping lane
fifteen minutes downstream from Belview Container
Terminal. On the alert for container ships, we kept out
of the central, deeper, channel. The river split around
Little Island, Queen's Channel to starboard, King's

Channel to port. We took the shorter Queen's, then paused as we heard news of the first tall ship. We had to wait now, allowing the main events to pass, so huddled on the edge of the river, had our lunch with an eye on the bend downstream, until, in the distance, we saw the mast tops moving first to left, then to right. We lined the decks of our boats in anticipation and, as it came round the corner, there was a collective gasp. It was the mighty Russian ship *Mir*, and we felt absolutely tiny as we hooted our horns. The ship hooted back and Russian sailors waved.

'I can hear drums,' I said a while later.

'Don't be silly. There's nowhere they could be playing drums.' We listened.

Another set of masts wound its way towards us. Drumbeats – they were certainly drumbeats – pulsed. The ship appeared, drummers on deck, and the hairs rose on the back of my neck. The ship's name said *Dewaruci*. It was from Indonesia.

Several ships later came the message via VHF that we could head to our berth. A small anxiety had crept in. After the long journey, would our place in the mud be satisfactory, or would we have to go back to St Mullins? The heavy barges with their flat bottoms could sit on mud without too much worry, at least if they were on their own. But a whole flotilla, joined up together and settling on deep mud that possibly hid broken metal waiting to puncture the skin of even a steel boat?

Our berth was round the corner from the Waterford Boat Club, at the point where St John's River flowed into the Suir. Two of our craft were given leave to tie up at the Boat Club jetty, but not for long. We were tolerated visitors only – there was some understandable resentment at our presence. Every native craft had been ordered to leave the Waterford area to make way for the tall ships, but we had been granted our place on the mud against all the odds. The HBA had convinced the organisers that *Irish* heritage boats should be part of a national heritage event set in Ireland.

It took a while to arrange ourselves next to a railing on the corner. The big canal boats were first in as always, providing a solid base for the rest. We were last, allocated a place at the edge of the bunched-up flotilla so we wouldn't dry out as the tide ebbed. There was a skippers' briefing on one of the barges, and it was here we learned how risky this whole enterprise was.

'We don't know what's going to happen when the tide goes out,' we were told. Each skipper would have to make their own call. There were risks not only from objects in the mud but also from boats pulling cleats off each other when they settled. It was a sombre party that went thoughtfully back to the still-floating boats.

In the end, everyone stayed where they were, tied up against each other, except for Rachel on her vintage Dutch barge. She moved a little up John's River, confident that she and her crew would be able to get themselves ashore without the bridge of barges. Then the wait began for the tide to go out. We were subdued, anxious, but also excited about our enviable view of the tall ships in the harbour. Small forays ashore showed us the buzz about town. Boards were set up next to the boats explaining who we were and giving information about the different vessels. We began to sink inexorably. Too late to change our minds now. Someone tied a plank from the railings on the increasingly high stone quay wall to the coach-house roof of the nearest barge. I tried not to think about walking across it.

Small boats were aground in St John's River and the tide was ebbing at speed. Soon Rachel's boat was in the mud. Everyone was quiet, waiting, holding their breath. The barges with the deepest draught began to settle. Ropes creaked in the cool evening air as smaller, outer boats tilted in unfamiliar ways. There were flurries of activity as fenders were dropped between rails and hulls as they leaned into each other. The last channels of water ran through the glistening mud. Some people would be sleeping at strange angles that would change every night as the tide went out, but for now things seemed to be OK. A hum of chatter rose over this odd-looking company of timber and steel, cruiser and barge.

When the tide was out, and we had to get the dogs off, we crept ashore via a couple of timber cruisers linked to the Boat Club jetty. This exit had been agreed for those with small children. Dogs weren't mentioned. However, once Aoife and Frankie were back on board it was The Plank. We clambered across decks to the barge nearest the wall, then onto its coach-house roof. One end of the plank rested here, the other on the metal rung of a ladder that climbed the quay wall. A rope 'handrail' had been set up, but nothing could avert one's (my) attention from the narrowness of the

plank and the hideous drop to the mud below. I am
one of those people who, when halfway across, say, a
log over a stream, will freeze midpoint and have to be
coaxed off, eyes closed and tearful. I whimpered gently as I put my foot onto the splinter of wood. There
was plenty of encouragement. It was the desire to not
appear a big girl's blouse that finally made me march
smartly across, gulp as I put my foot on the ladder and
clamber up the seemingly endless rungs to grasp the
solidity of the rail at the top.

There were two ways to tour the tall ships. One
was via quay walls and floating jetties that allowed
access to the ships. The other was by boat. Several
times over the next couple of days we slid into the
river, our guests on board, glasses in hand to get up
close at hull level. Everyone with access to a small boat
was doing the same. There was great pride in the two
Irish ships, the *Jeanie Johnston* and the *Asgard II*. A fun-
fair on the quay added to the carnival air, its big wheel
dwarfed by metres-high masts. Fireworks on Friday
night finished the festival.

We were woken by talking. It was impossibly early
– the night before had only just ended. Someone
sounded a horn. Joe and I opened the hatch in the fore
cabin and stuck our heads out. Seven o'clock, and the
first tall ship was sailing past, setting out on the first leg
of the race to Cherbourg. We made it onto the deck,
waking our friend Jean still curled up in the saloon,
Aoife asleep in the crook of her legs. The Indonesian
ship won the prize again for most arresting. This time

they weren't only drumming – the crew in ceremonial dress of navy shirt and white trousers were ranged along the yardarms and snagged in the rigging, undulating long, red ribbons in time to the rhythms drifting from the deck far below. It was like the floor section of an Olympic gymnastics contest taking place up the masts of a ship.

That afternoon we moved our boats to the floating jetties recently vacated by the tall ships. Such luxury – we and the dogs could get on and off the boat without clambering or walking the plank. Security fencing and gate protected the jetties and their boats from the road, and many of us planned to leave our vessels here for another week while we went home. Then it would be back to St Mullins and non-tidal waters.

Chapter Ten

*F*our boats rafted up, at anchor in Dollar Bay in the Suir Estuary. A scorching day. We stood on the sandy bottom, the lap of little waves round our shoulders, alongside dogs whose dignity had been compromised as they were lowered off the aft deck. We half waded, half swam, the dogs beside us. They paddled ashore easily, shaking their heads and licking unfamiliar salt from their lips. Freshwater dogs, these.

It was the day after the tall ships left. The forecast was settled, so we'd taken the chance to go into the estuary. Two of our boats had been on the Shannon Estuary trip, and we had depth sounders and appropriate charts between us. We felt a great sense of freedom after the confines of our mud berth and whipped along with the tide, out past Cheekpoint and into new territory. We were cruising happily, travelling at speed (for us) when Joe called out 'What's that?' pointing at a small buoy. Buoys can make you nervous when you're not sure what they are marking, but we were well within the channel. Then we noticed *Vicki May*, another timber cruiser, turning suddenly. Message on the VHF from Carson on *Blackslee*. Fishing nets. Jesus. The little coloured buoys were stretched across the channel and we were racing towards them with the outgoing tide. I did a reverse and turn to starboard manoeuvre. It was not very dignified, but the idea of getting a fisherman's net caught round the prop was not enticing. A boat without steerage in a strong tidal flow was terrifying, but even more upsetting would be the shame of showing oneself up as an amateur. Unnerved, I put on plenty of power, glad of the two engines, and found the open channel to the right. I imagined the contempt of Waterford fishermen watching us.

Our four small boats began to feel ever smaller. Ahead was the car ferry connecting Passage East to Ballyhack, and immediately after that the river opened out. The water was calm and very blue, with plenty of room to avoid shipping. We motored on, checking the chart, checking our depth against the chart to make sure we were where we thought we were, looking out for somewhere to stop. In the distance a couple of boats pulled out from a bay far in to the left. The chart told us this was Dollar Bay, and near the shore was a depth of between one and two metres. This could be our place. We altered course, picked a spot and cruised until we could drop anchors to the sandy seabed. I couldn't wait to get into the water. A haze shimmered. Small ripples appeared and disappeared with the faint breeze. We all hurried into our swimming togs. Down the ladder into warm water. Warm! Unbelievable. The Irish Riviera.

There was no land access to the little sandy cove. The dogs sniffed about, tongues drooping from the sides of their mouths. I skimmed stones across the unruffled water, knee deep. We paddled about, soaking in the heat, then swam back to the boats and the challenge of getting dogs on board. Aoife was easy – Joe could lift her small weight above his head, but Frankie? Oh dear. Poor dog was not happy, hauled up awkwardly by her harness, pushed by Joe below and pulled by me onto the deck.

That evening the other three boats returned to Waterford, but we needed to go home for a few days and decided to leave *Winter Solstice* above the lock in St Mullins. We turned right under Barrow Bridge at 5.30 and went with the incoming tide as far as New Ross. Things had improved – the new floating jetties were connected to land. The boat-length pontoons were arranged at right angles off central walkways, like opposing leaves off a stalk. The tide was coming in, and as it's easier to control a boat *against* the flow, we were looking for a gap on the upstream side so we could reverse in. But even better! There was space on the outside and I could practice ferry gliding.

I'd been told the principle of ferry gliding some years before, but had never had such a flow on a river in which to perfect the skill. It's an impressive manoeuvre. You bring your boat alongside a jetty or quay wall, then float sideways, apparently by magic, into place. Anyone who's been on a river ferry will have experienced this – which is why, of course, it's called ferry gliding. For maximum effect, nonchalantly approach a tight space between two boats on quay wall or jetty. An audience is good as long as you're confident. When parallel to the gap, steady the boat against the current until your position is held. Turn the wheel towards the jetty and, if you have twin engines, give a few more revs on the 'outer' engine. The boat crabs into its berth.

Next morning we left New Ross just after 9 a.m., arriving at the Scar in St Mullins at 10.45. The tide was in, the water high, and fifteen minutes later we were through the lock, tucking *Winter Solstice* into a space between two cruisers.

Our tall ships flotilla had split and scattered about the Barrow and Suir. Arriving back in New Ross a few days later, we found several flotilla boats moored at the jetties. We had plans to return to the estuary while the weather was fine, and discovered we would not be alone – the boats at New Ross, and most of those still in Waterford, were on their way there too. A jolly party turned left under Barrow Bridge at Cheekpoint, where others joined us from Waterford. We looked out for fishing nets but there were none. It was a breezy day, but sunny. At Ballyhack the river broadened, turned a little to the south, and suddenly the wind was on the nose. We paused, all of us, and milled around considering our options. We could see white horses ahead – a wind-over-tide effect making a force three to four seem more like a five or six. The difficulty was not with boating skills but with boats: flat-bottomed craft designed for the canal roll in even the gentlest swell. We volunteered to go ahead and see what it was like simply because *Winter Solstice*, although not a big craft, was designed for coastal waters. We didn't have company. It was choppy out there and we found ourselves rearing and dropping over the waves, so sent word back, kept going as far as Duncannon and eased into its sheltered harbour to wait for the tide to turn.

That night we stayed in Passage East, where the ferry crosses to Ballyhack. The small fishing harbour emptied of water when the tide went out, but there was a quay wall, which, it was decided, would do us for the night. Barges in first. The small boats waited, circling, rafting up with each other. After a while *Blackslee* cut away back to Waterford, tired of waiting. We nearly did the same, but then were called into place at the outside of the raft.

The ferry sailed from 7 a.m. to 10 p.m. It crossed the river, emptied itself of vehicles, refilled its decks, crossed back. As it pulled into its dock it set up a wave that washed into our foolish little raft of boats. Ropes creaked with the pressure put on them. Deck cleats took the strain, as we were tied to each other as well as to land. And a rude awakening at 7 a.m. Oh dear. We couldn't believe it when most of the others said they were going to stay another night. We were off back to Waterford with ideas of going the other way, upstream to Carrick-on-Suir.

To get to Carrick, you have to be certain of your timing. Once the tide goes out, although the jetty there has a good level of water, the area around it does not. We worked out how long it would take, checked the tide charts and decided we should leave by 11.15.

Chatting to others on the Waterford pontoons that morning raised an interest. Soon we had a crowd going upriver – three cruisers, one small barge and ourselves.

'We just have to do a quick car shuttle,' said one member of the proposed flotilla. 'Won't be long'. Boat trips were often punctuated by 'car shuttles', where two cars travelled to the boat destination, one was left, and two drivers returned to the starting point.

Eventually we left at 12.30. Still OK as long as we got a move on. But we didn't get a move on. It was a very pretty river lined with trees. There was the distraction of the Waterford and Suir Valley narrow-gauge railway, whose locomotive and period carriages ran alongside, a charity affair run by volunteers and taking in 17 km of scenic countryside. The original railway opened in 1878, was 43 miles (69 km) long and ran from Waterford to Dungarvan. The main shareholder was the Duke of Devonshire. His family seat was Lismore Castle, where there happened to be a very handy railway station.

High tide at Carrick was at 14.38. There was little leeway either side of this to get into the jetty without going aground. We decided to put our foot down a bit. Not everyone did the same. It was 15.15 when we pulled into Carrick, and the water was emptying out fast. *Blackslee* and *Sin É* tied up with little time to spare. The fourth cruiser came under the bridge, a notorious sticking spot, without trouble, but then went too far to the left. Suddenly it was going nowhere, and unkind words drifted across the water. Those of us already moored walked along the jetty, wondering what advice to give, when the skipper hopped over-board, the crew lamenting how he'd surely drown. The water came up to his waist.

With judicious use of ropes and brute force the cruiser was rocked off her sandbank and pulled, com-plaining, to a mooring. The small barge was not so lucky. Bringing up the rear in stately fashion, and with a deeper draught than the cruisers, she stuck fast under the bridge. That would be it until the tide released her in the early hours of the morning.

Carrick's original name was Carrig Mac Griffin (or Carrickmagriffin), which I rather like. Perhaps Joe had relatives there on his father's side. He certainly had them on his mother's side, her family coming from upstream in Clonmel. Horse-drawn boats used to nav-igate the river as far as Clonmel, although it wasn't an easy passage, with many weirs and rapids, and at Sir Thomas's Bridge, built without a towpath, the poor horses had to join the boat in the water, no mean feat when the river was in spate.

It's possible that Anne Boleyn, very likely the most famous beheadee in English history, was born in Carrick. Her mother Margaret, daughter of the seventh Earl of Ormond, was known to have visited her family in Tipperary, and there's a story that this is where she gave birth to Anne. There's no formal record of Anne's birth, so why not? It was well after this, however, that 'Black Tom' Butler, the tenth Earl of Ormond, built the new Ormond Castle in 1565. This beautiful build-ing is not a castle at all, having no fortifications, but instead is a Tudor manor house with steep gables and mullioned windows, rooms lined with oak panels and carved limestone.

The Castle is open to the public – it was taken over in 1947 and restored by the State – so we went to have a look. There's a decoration there displaying the initials T.O. (Thomas Ormond) and E.R. (Elizabeth Regina), said to be an indication of the warm relationship between Tom and Elizabeth I. Some say it was a romantic attachment, while others argue it was a strong friendship of mutual respect. There's no definite proof either way, but Tom certainly hoped Elizabeth would visit his glorious creation. Elizabeth used to call him her 'black husband', probably because of his swarthy complexion and black hair: Thomas Carte, the eighteenth-century biographer, described Ormond as:

> …a man of very great parts, admirable judgment, great experience, and a prodigious memory; … very comely and graceful, of a black complexion which gave occasion to the Queen (in her way of expressing kindness to such as she favoured) to call him her 'black husband'.

Elizabeth never did visit Ormond Castle.

★★★

I eased myself down the transom ladder. It was time for a wash, and the river water, though clear as a rain-drop, was cold, oh so cold, as I hung down from the rungs, iciness up as far as my waist. Then I let go, out into the stream, swimming frantically before calling Joe a coward for not coming in. The shampoo sat on the aft deck. Once the water seemed warm I reached for it and lathered up, then ducked under to rinse.

St Mullins became our second home that summer, a haven just above the tide filled with sunshine. Some weekends we stayed put, varnishing the boat, struggling to find shade, chatting to other boaters, walking the towpath and the woods. The only difficulty was water. The Barrow has very few taps for boaters, and the closest to us was in the graveyard in the village of St Mullins, a good enough walk if you were carrying heavy containers. Drinking water was doable – we brought several ten-litre containers from home. But water-tank water, if we had any at all, was heavily rationed. You have a different relationship with water – and washing – if it's not easily available. When you have to fetch water for a strip wash or jump into a freezing river you quickly realise you don't 'need' to shower every day in a climate like ours. After a while there's a certain liberation to going grubby, or just washing the bits that matter.

Every so often we left our cosy canal-side berth. In the middle of August we studied our tide charts and set forth. The lock gates opened to reveal the tidal river, and *Winter Solstice* moved out slowly into the stream, cruising carefully across the Scar, keeping to the St Mullins side where the steamers used to go. We were on our way to the third 'Sister', the River Nore, and the village of Inistioge at the end of its tidal waters. We'd already been there by car. At Inistioge you either have to dry out against the wall or stay in the deep pool in the middle of the river – the tide is in for only a few hours a day.

Our drive to the village had shown us the possibilities of that wall. There were a couple of boats leaning into it, one with a fellow underneath painting on the anti-foul paint that, he said, would be dry by the time the tide came in. Joe had ideas. Couldn't we do the same? We'd never dried out in *Winter Solstice* before, but in principle it would work. She had a very solid keel, we were pretty sure she'd dried out in her previous incarnation as a coastal and estuary boat, and it would save us the difficulties and cost of having her taken out of the water.

We had to make the journey in two stages to work the tides. We left St Mullins on Thursday evening, and passed under Ferrymountgarret with six inches to spare between our roof and the bridge. The Nore entered the Barrow on the right some ten minutes later, but the tide was ebbing. Even if we pushed *Winter Solstice* upriver against the flow, we would run out of depth well before reaching Inistioge, so we continued a little further downstream to New Ross. The following evening high tide in Inistioge would be at 19.45, so we left New Ross at 17.20. We still hadn't definitely decided to dry out, but the idea of ferrying dogs to shore in the dinghy wasn't appealing – memories of hauling Frankie aboard in Dollar Bay. We'd see how it looked when we got there and, indeed, see if there was room. Just before 7 p.m. we came round a big bend in the river with plenty of depth beneath the hull, left Gowlaun Island to port, and saw one boat moored on the wall. That gave us encouragement – we wouldn't be alone in drying out. We'd take a chance.

The tide turned just as *The Bat*, an old canal barge, chugged into the pool in the middle of the river. On *Winter Solstice* we laid our anchor chain along the starboard side deck to encourage her to lean into the wall when her keel touched bottom and she no longer had the support of water. I whispered to her that it would all be OK, she mustn't worry. The water began to drop, imperceptibly at first, then the ebb of the tide joined with the flow of the river and you could see the water falling almost as though you were in a canal lock. We fussed anxiously from shore and boat, watching for the first tilt. There it was. She went aground and listed slightly to starboard, resting her shoulder against the quay wall, taking the weight off her keel as though she'd been doing this all her life.

Soon there was a narrow channel on the other side of what had been a broad stretch of river. Beneath *Winter Solstice,* vegetation was growing. But for the puddles, it would be hard to believe there had ever been water here, never mind enough to float a boat. *The Bat* had its dinghy out and crew were coming ashore. There was a mere few metres of water to cross from the pool where they were anchored. A stony beach appeared. Our boat seemed so solidly settled that we left her and went to the pub.

Early next morning I half woke, aware we were no longer at an angle, surprised I'd slept so well on a tilt.

I was thankful that *Winter Solstice* had a holding tank so we could use the toilet without unpleasant consequences below. It felt good to be level again, to feel the movement of a floating boat. Not for long, though. After breakfast we watched again as the keel took the weight, and we settled once more onto the riverbed. Time to get busy. As soon as the hull was dry – not long, as the sun was splitting the stones again – we began cleaning and doing small repair jobs by sanding and filling and quickly stroking on a bit of paint.

I was taking a break, walking along the quay with the dogs and letting them into the water via the slipway to cool off. Aoife had been doing her usual barking into her reflection while splashing with her front legs, but suddenly she was standing on the slip looking odd. She was hunched, and her back leg was straight out behind her. Then she staggered. I ran down to her. She was disorientated and her legs were doing odd things. Then she couldn't stand. I picked her up and walked quickly back to the boat, calling Joe. I felt sick. We had no car, didn't know anyone here. We grabbed the dog leads (mostly for Frankie) and half ran to the village, which was five minutes away from the bridge below which we were moored. I sat on the sweet-smelling grass of the village green, Aoife on my lap, while Joe went to try and find the number of a vet. I still felt sick. Aoife still looked sick. We were afraid of poison. Dogs are dreadful scavengers, and that morning she'd found something in the hedgerow near the boat, eaten before we could see what it was. Maybe it was poisoned meat. Or badly gone-off meat harbouring some dreadful disease. Or maybe rat poison had been put down. Imagination can be a terrible thing.

A vet was recommended to Joe by a woman in a shop, and he phoned him. He would come to us, but would be at least half an hour. The wait was ghastly. Aoife seemed to rally at one point, and we took her to the water to cool off, feeling relief, wondering whether to cancel the vet, but then it happened again.

The vet said that poison was a possibility. All he could do in that case, he said, was take her to his surgery and put her on a drip. However, he warned, it was probably too late for such treatment to do much as any poison would have been absorbed already. He wasn't convinced that was the case anyway as Aoife had perked up again, showing an interest, starting to be bold. In the end we took her back to the boat, coddled and fussed her and watched for a recurrence of scary symptoms. It didn't happen.

We never quite got to the bottom of Aoife's funny turn. But she did have a couple more, again while on the boat (typical). We didn't panic as much, but brought her to our own vet once we got home. He suspected she was having mini fits. Idiopathic, he called them, which meant the cause was unknown. If she continued having them he would suggest medication, but she didn't. They stopped completely. As our hearts almost had.

The second day in Inistioge was a Friday, and so lovely we decided to stay. Beside the quay were a couple of closely mown, flat areas of grass, and late that afternoon three carloads of campers arrived. Two tents were pitched just beyond our boat and another couple at the end nearest the slip. There was a party atmosphere as, once unpacked, they lit their barbecues. At about 6.30 p.m., *Winter Solstice* went afloat again and we watched the river climbing the wall. It was a spring tide so would be high. The day before the water had come just over the top of the quay to lap across the tarmac for a metre or so. Today's tide would be even higher. We were about to experience the effect of syzygy. Syzygy is not a rock band specialising in ornate gyrations but an alignment of three celestial objects – the sun, the earth and, in the case of tides, the moon.

Every day the tide goes in and out twice, and sometimes is higher than others. Tides occur when the moon tries to pull the water off the earth with its gravity, but the earth hangs on tight. The result is a bulge in the ocean that we experience as a rising of the water level. When the sun joins in as well, i.e., when you have syzygy, this bulge becomes even bigger and is known as a spring tide. Springs occur when the moon is either full or new, and in alignment with the sun. Neap tides, on the other hand, happen when the sun and moon are not aligned but are at right angles to each other in relation to the earth; at quarter moon, in other words. With neaps, both high and low tide are more moderate than springs. Sometimes you get an unusually high spring tide, for example when you have a new moon that is particularly close to the earth. We were about to experience such an event.

When *Winter Solstice* was resting her midships against the quay, our boarding-plank was more or less horizontal. As the tide came in, the end on the aft deck began to rise. Water tipped over the top of the wall. Joe and I sat on our folding chairs with a cup of tea to watch. Smoke rose from the barbecues on the grass. The water sprawled towards us.

'That's beyond where it came to yesterday,' I said, getting up for a closer look – tides coming in need watching. It was spreading quickly now across the gentle slope of tarmac. Soon we wouldn't be able to get back on board without getting our feet wet.

'Mm,' said Joe. We looked at each other, went into the cockpit, took out the wellies and put them on, paddled to our folding chairs and moved them back a metre. The barbecues were gingerly lifted closer to the tents. Aoife mooched happily in the water. We moved the chairs again. Water oozed across the grassy areas. Then we saw the trip boat from New Ross rounding the corner, a fair old bow wave sending wash into the riverbank. There was sudden tent activity. Pegs were pulled and one tent was lifted, contents and all, to the slightly higher ground at the edge of the grassy patch. The barbecue went too. The other tent was raised up and carried to the far end of the quay where it was still dry. The trip boat kept coming at speed (tut-tut). We paddled to *Winter Solstice*, suddenly anxious she would be washed ashore, leaning our weight onto her as the wash whooshed.

At one of these unusually high tides a narrowboat had come upriver, but instead of stopping at the wall or in the pool it carried on under the bridge (the end of navigation) and tied to a tree on the edge of the village. The tide quickly went out, as it does, and the narrowboat settled onto the riverbed. Not a problem for a flat-bottomed boat. It was, so the story goes, three months before it floated again.

We woke to Saturday morning drizzle. Perhaps it was just as well, otherwise we might never have escaped this enchanted place. Once the decision was made to go there was no time to linger. We pulled away from our wall just before 9 a.m., and cruised slowly down to New Ross on the ebbing tide.

Chapter Eleven

*S*ummer again, heading north to Lough Erne but taking our time, pottering up from Lough Derg through Banagher and Shannonbridge, pausing in Athlone to visit our friend Rachel, tying up outside Abbey House with its garden onto the Shannon before crossing Lough Ree. Halfway up the lake we turned into Blackbrink Bay, the site of our breakdown aboard the Emerald Star hire boat. From there we took the canal to Lecarrow, seeking stillness in the tiny backwater. There were a few boats moored when we arrived. We pulled into a spot at the end of the stone quay and let the dogs off for their first excitable sniff.

'Oh we're *here*,' they said.

It wasn't raining. In fact we were having some beautiful weather, so Joe lit the barbecue as I peeled potatoes. Looking out of the galley window I saw a three-storey boat glide into the harbour. The peeler stilled in my hand, the potato dropped into the water as the boat came towards me, stopping just in time directly behind us. High on its fly bridge was the skipper, and above him, attached to an arch, were receivers for radar and GPS. A satellite dish for television. A long aerial for VHF radio. Good grief.

Another one came into view, equally tall and broad, and rafted off the first. I was amazed these things could get down the canal. Glad we didn't meet one coming the other way. Then a third, and my view of the harbour disappeared. An instant block of flats had been installed in our back garden. We could hear (but couldn't see) another raft of similar boats forming behind the first. I went ashore to join Joe and watch the proceedings. Boat crew bustled, lowering fenders covered in their own socks, navy knitted affairs to keep the fenders clean and protect the boat from something called 'fender scuff', a sickness I can't say I've noticed. Skippers looked down from their steering eyries.

Activity passed to the various poop decks, high-up outdoor platforms at the rear of the boats, all furnished with tables, chairs and sun umbrellas. Gas bottles were attached to patio barbecues, ignitions pressed and the smell of burning steaks wafted along the harbour.

'Come far?' I asked the man looking down on us from next door.

'Quigley's at Killinure. D'you know it?'

'Yes indeed. The inner lakes are lovely aren't they?'

'Nowhere better.'

'Take you long to get here?'

'Half an hour. We took it easy.'

'So are you off on a trip up the river?'

'Oh no. We'll go back to the marina tomorrow. We're just up here for the night.'

This was when it really hit me how things had changed on the river. I should have realised it already. I'd had a conversation with a new boat owner in Terryglass at the top of Lough Derg. It started in the predictable way as I took his ropes.

'Come far?'

'Tarmonbarry,' he said. 'We just went up there for lunch.'

'Sorry? You went there and back today?'

'We did. Couldn't get any further because of the bridge.'

I was unable to say much else because of the shock. According to my boat's log it took us just over nine hours to get to Tarmonbarry, and we did that over four days, stopping in harbours along the way. And this man had been there for lunch? How many cups of tea were spilled and binoculars thrown to the floor as he ploughed his way along? This was the type of fellow responsible for my anxiety about boats coming from behind on narrow sections of river. The bow wave off a craft coming towards you is easy to deal with, however big, as you simply turn to catch the wave at a ninety-degree angle. From behind, though, it's another matter. After being caught broadside a couple of times with tables and dogs pitching about in the ensuing wash, I'd taken to stopping *Winter Solstice* altogether and turning her stern to take the wave – a quicker manoeuvre than turning her bow. But this needed planning, and some of these boats moved so fast you hadn't time to act. It was, I must add, against the Shannon Navigation byelaws to travel up the river at this sort of speed.

These fast boats were increasingly causing a problem for wildlife, particularly in spring when waterfowl built their nests in the reeds along the bank. Wash from one of these speeding vessels could lift the nest clear of the water, depositing it and its cargo of eggs or chicks into the river to disappear downstream on the current. Fishermen standing in open lake boats were vulnerable too, at risk of being toppled.

It was speed for the sake of it. The 'boaters' we met in Lecarrow rarely travelled far. Their cruisers were holiday cottages, an escape from the city. Not a cheap option though, as some of these cruisers cost more than a three-bedroom house. In spring 2007, a brokerage company was advertising boats (45 ft in length) that cost over €400,000 and these were second-hand. A 35-foot, 'budget-priced' boat was €166,500. Mooring costs for a 45-footer can add an annual cost of up to €3,000.

It had become fashionable to own an 'offshore' boat with two engines (twin-screw cruisers), designed for open water and high speed, another must-have accessory for the newly moneyed. These craft had radar, VHF and satellite navigation so they could take their owners to France and Spain or across the North Sea to Holland. There were similar boats available with single engines designed for the inland waterways, but they didn't have the required cachet among a certain breed of boater. Long-established boat builders Broom, for example, produced a vessel specifically for the Shannon with accommodation almost identical to that of the offshore version. A twin-screw cruiser that rarely went to sea had to contend with shallow waters on a navigation designed for boats of limited draught. The offshore hull offered no protection to rudder and propeller as it was designed for a different purpose – to get the craft onto the plane (nose in the air, bottom down) as soon as a critical speed was reached. The propeller, and the shaft that drove it, would need replacing if a crunch against a rock twisted them out of shape. A lucrative source of revenue for boatyard managers: it could cost €45,000 to sort out damage to the wrong boat on the wrong waterway.

That was their problem. The problem for the rest of us was that they couldn't go slowly enough for river work – to go at speeds required on the inland waterways they would lose steerage. We were glad to escape into the north Shannon from this strange new world: not far from the top of Lough Ree the river passes through Tarmonbarry, where our Terryglass friend had gone for lunch. There's a lock here, which is fine for ocean cruisers, then a lifting bridge, which is not, as it won't lift high enough for these big boats, even when their superstructures are folded down. There was another such bridge at Rooskey, further north still. A sanctuary from offshore speed.

We'd heard talk of a fabulous Lebanese restaurant in Jamestown, a tiny village on a bend of the Shannon in Co. Leitrim. Unlikely as this seemed, we planned to investigate. We came up through Albert Lock in late afternoon. Beside us rose a boat of similar size to *Winter Solstice* called *Elsewhere,* and its skipper looked familiar. It was Dick Warner, the broadcaster and waterways enthusiast, and he too had thoughts of Lebanese cuisine. For those unfamiliar with such food, the speciality is a *meze*, a series of tiny dishes served up over an evening. To fully benefit from this feast you need a few people – in fact the more the better so you can order a bigger *meze* with a greater variety of dishes to taste. Joe was cheering up. He knew that a *meze* was hopeless (or certainly not value for money) with me as I'm full after the first couple of courses, but with five people … We decided we would go together, Dick, his wife and son and us.

The restaurant was an unusual mix of Lebanese decoration and Irish bungalow. The outside was completely unremarkable, but inside you were carried at least halfway to the shores of the Mediterranean with whitewashed walls, clever lighting, wooden tables and authentic food prepared by the Lebanese chef. We had the fullest *meze*, seventeen courses, and it was very late when we left. Plans to visit a boating friend were abandoned.

A gentle start next morning, leaving Jamestown mid-morning for Leitrim Village, where we planned to leave the boat for a few days. Coming into Leitrim we were surprised by major construction work. Edging the waterway just beyond the point where the Shannon forks to the left was a building with the feeling of a mill, several storeys tall in grey stone. It advertised itself as a unique waterfront development of luxury apartments.

'Who's going to live there?' I said.

'People working in Carrick?' said Joe doubtfully. But that wasn't all.

'Bloody hell,' I said. There were more apartments gathered round a marina – a private marina – and a hotel! In Leitrim? What was going on? We motored towards the stone bridge in shocked silence.

'We can tie to the bank if the jetty's full,' said Joe as we passed under the arch. But there was no bank. It had been cut away for another private marina and associated apartments. There was a line of floating jetties on the river bank too, but they were taped off with a sign saying no mooring, and there was no land bridge, so you couldn't get ashore unless you happened to have packed your stilts. This apartment block didn't even try to look water-related. Built of concrete blocks, it resembled the tackiest type of urban development. What was it doing blighting a tiny place like Leitrim?

It was lunchtime by the time we arrived at Drumshanbo Lock, and we were happy to sit in the sun and eat our sandwiches, but now it was gone 2 p.m. We shouted into the speaker built into the wall of the lock building and asked for the lock-keeper to let us through. Twice. Three times. Another boat joined us, *Little Phoenix*, a small but very sweet timber sailing boat with skipper Andrew and his dog on board. Time was getting on and it was difficult to curb our impatience. I had in mind a swim and wanted the heat of the early afternoon to encourage me to take the plunge. Joe can never bear waiting too long for anything. Andrew was probably the most sanguine among us by the time the lock-keeper turned up at nearly 3 p.m. The joys of slow boating.

The lock fed us into the expanse of Lough Allen, the northernmost navigable water on the Shannon. We were watched over by mountains on all sides. On the right *Sliabh an Iarainn*, the Iron Mountains; up ahead on the Cavan-Fermanagh border the Cuilcagh Mountains; to our left Arigna with its isolated villages and remains of the Arigna mines. Lough Allen opened to commercial boats when the Lough Allen Canal, bypassing rapids between Battlebridge and Drumshanbo, opened in 1817. The driving force behind the canal was the need to transport coal extracted from these mines.

Arigna coal was accessed not through shafts but via tunnels known as roads that ran into the mountain. To we pampered people today their lifestyle seems impossibly hard – well, it was impossibly hard, but that was the way things were, and, like people everywhere, they found a sense of pride and community in what they were doing.

You can visit the mines today and be taken through the dripping tunnels to experience something of what it might have been like, though thankfully avoiding the more claustrophobic passages. The tunnels that led off the main, pin-straight road were only high enough for a small man to squeeze into. Each man would work towards another – that was decided between them – until they met in the middle. That way there was the same amount of coal available to each – important, as you were paid according to what you produced.

It would probably be the rats, not the small spaces, that would repulse many, but they were viewed with tolerance, if not respect, as although you would have to put up with them using you as a walkway while you lay there chipping coal, they provided an early warning system for poisonous gas in the mine – Arigna canaries. They also kept the latrines clean, but we won't go into that one.

We kept to the western side of the lake, *en route* to Spencer Harbour, where we'd stopped four years previously with the HBA. *Little Phoenix* kept to the east, heading for Cleighran More. As we turned left at the top of the lake we could see the harbour ahead. Empty. We pulled in quickly and got into our swimming togs, then waded into the shallow (and *warm*) sandy entry, just the business for Joe, who likes to keep in his depth, and for me as I'm a wimp at getting in.

By evening we'd been joined by a couple of other boats plus some local teenage boys and girls playing music on what we used to call a ghetto blaster, the boys bombing into the water in a misguided attempt to impress the girls. On leaving, they carefully put their Coke bottles and various wrappers in a pile, presumably for the bin men to collect. To be fair, the girls went and picked them up to bring away when I asked them – poor things. Such a loss of cool.

We'd never been to Cleighran More, the harbour on the east of the lake, largely because it had only recently been attached to the land. Although remaining still and calm, the previous day's sunshine had given way to an overcast of grey. We passed the End of Navigation, where the baby Shannon enters the lake, and I thought of the swim I would have in spite of the dull skies. This harbour, like Spencer, was nearly empty, except for *Little Phoenix*. No gentle sandy bay though – the bit-of-a-beach was rocky and grey as the sky. I could have gone in off the back of the boat, but a hopeful dip of fingers in the water was not encouraging. It would have to be the beach. Joe was persuaded to come too, but this wasn't to be a swimming day for him. The water was *so* cold. It wasn't the lack of sunshine – a sunny day only makes you think it's warmer. We may as well have been wading into a different lake than yesterday's. Eventually I swam out gasping, trying to persuade Joe it was warm once you were in, but I was lying. It was simply that I'd gone numb. I must have been swimming in water directly from the nascent Shannon; in other words, an icy mountain stream.

A couple of hours later, when the sun finally found its way through the clouds and the crew from two more boats were strolling around in t-shirts, I was still wrapped in multiple layers of wool and fleece. The sky was flaming, taking on a startling shade of tangerine. It began to resemble a bad painting of a sunset from an artist with only a child's palette of paints and no notion of how to mix. Our stretch of jetty became a viewing platform. We unfolded our camping chairs for the show, set up the little slatted-wood table, poured out glasses of chilled white and turned golden in the glow. The water rippled its orangeness towards us while the sun sank behind the mountains in a most un-Irish show of colour. I felt almost warm in its reflection.

We needed to kill time after Lough Allen. There was to be a shindig in Jamestown at the weekend. Cormac Kenny, owner of canal boat *76M* (of Harvey Wallbanger fame), lived in Jamestown, where they held an annual show. In 2006, the organisers, Cormac included, decided it would be a splendid idea to re-erect the arch of the old town gate in the middle of the village and invite a rake of heritage boats to support the event. The arch would need re-erecting as it had lost its head – not, as one might expect of a seventeenth-century structure, to a rampaging army but damaged by a 1970s lorry. Cormac had persuaded us to come along as a representative of classic timber craft. So we went to Lough Key and Boyle for a few days.

It was hot. So hot. There was no shelter in Boyle Harbour, but Joe was determined to take advantage of the dry weather to put another coat of varnish on the coach-house sides. The dogs and I sheltered under a golf umbrella until he was finished and we could escape. We didn't go far – just to the stretch of Boyle River between Lough Key and the short Boyle Canal. Tied to the bank, we hurried into the bliss of cold water, dogs too. I dived off the aft deck. We sat half submerged on the bank, then drank cold beer in the cockpit until the heat went out of the day and we could face the harbour again.

Next day was just as hot. We left Boyle mid-morning and stopped for lunch in Knockvicar. A quick swim. All the local children were in and out of the water, swinging from a rope and letting go. Then Cootehall. People were swimming before the bridge off great slabs of rock and we couldn't wait to join them.

It was later, walking the dogs in the cool of the evening, that we realised it wasn't just Leitrim Village that was full of building equipment – Cootehall, too, had succumbed to the building boom. A new estate was under construction on the big triangular field between church and river. Rows of identical semi-detached houses with little red-bricked drives. At the bridge a billboard detailed the deal – a free Maxum sports boat worth around €16,500 with every house. Just what the Shannon needed. A big sticker proclaimed SOLD OUT. We were told the SOLD OUT occurred off the plans on the day the houses came on the market.

Planning signs advised us there would be thirty-two more houses behind the pub near the river, fifteen on the other side of the bridge from our swimming spot and another six in the centre. The landlord of the waterside pub had sold some of his own land to developers. He objected when the plans were first put in, as had most of the village, but when building became inevitable he had taken his profit like everyone else. Cootehall was to become more housing estate than village.

★★★

In Jamestown there were eighty boats, forty of them heritage barges. You could walk from one side of the broad river to the other on boats. Townspeople came to us and we went to the townspeople. In particular we went to the Jamestown Show – the dog show bit. This was an arm-twisting job. Wandering around the show-ground with our dogs, and our friend Rachel with her dogs, a nice lady with a clipboard pounced. 'Will you enter the dog show? You'll enjoy it. Do your bit for the show.' The only pedigree among us was Rachel's pug, Polly. We entered Aoife and Frankie into three events – two for mongrel versions of their breed and one for the dog the judge – our nice clipboard lady, now looking rather fierce – would most like to take home. I was amazed the judge was taking it all seriously but Joe wasn't at all surprised. He knew about dog shows, having been a dog photographer in a previous life, and this was an event that qualified the winners for other shows, so boosting the price of their puppies.

Joe took Aoife and I took Frankie. Aoife thought it a hoot, barking and showing off. Every so often she took a roll round on the warm grass. She wasn't placed. Frankie's turn. She was looking peaky. I think she'd just been stung in her mouth by a wasp (not for the first time, having never connected the pain to stripey buzzy things). Unlike Aoife, she didn't enjoy herself at all, tail down, gloomy face. But she came second!

Polly the Pug was the star of the whole dog show, coming away with several firsts. The prizes were tins of dog food. The winner of the first class received half a dozen tins. By the final class they were giving away box-loads. You have a dog? Here, have some dog food. Sitting outside the pub that afternoon in celebration we discovered the tins were out of date. But only just. The dogs didn't mind.

★★★

Winter Solstice rocked from side to side, but at least there was no jagging on the cleats. We'd taken precautions this time on Lough Erne, fashioning a stretchy section on our ropes with bicycle inner tubes. There were two ways you could go on the river in 2006 – with or against the water sporters and speedboats. We were fed up with against, forever complaining about the influx of boats driven by people with a sudden flush of cash but little knowledge of the river. These boaters either didn't know or didn't care about slowing down as they passed a jetty, and we feared for our decks and our sanity. At Bun Bridge we hadn't expected to need our stretchy lines – we'd decided to go a twisty route on our way from Quivvy Marina to the Lower Lough, stopping at places we hadn't been before. Bun Bridge was one of them, a quiet spot (ha!) not far from Crom Castle.

It *was* Sunday afternoon, so a prime time for water sports, but this was something else. Wakeboarding had hit the waterways and it was certainly making waves. Where water-skiing boats skimmed the water the wakeboard craft had specially built ballast tanks to drop the stern low and produce a pair of big fat waves across which wake boarders could perform their tricks. We stopped at Bun Bridge in spite of all this a) because we were hungry and b) we were trying out our new everyone-has-a-right-to-the-waterway attitude, encouraged by the water-skiing family we'd met in Grange, a tiny place at the end of the Carnadoe waters off Lough Boderg, whose company we'd enjoyed and skills we'd admired.

We battened down the boat to avoid damage to its contents, had lunch and a glass of wine (that always helps in these situations) and sat on the jetty to watch (it was too bumpy on the boat). Conversation was sporadic, the powerful outboard motors being raucous, but it was entertaining enough, not so much because of the competent wakeboarding – there were as many beginners as experienced practitioners – but because of the interactions between people. People-watching with noise, action and colourful wetsuits.

It was as well there were things to watch as that was all I could do. Or at least I was limited in that I was on crutches. I had something called plantar fasciitis, a foot condition that causes pain in the heel. I could no longer walk any distance. My doctor had put me on a second course of anti-inflammatory drugs and said to not walk on the foot at all. The treatment didn't seem to be making any difference, the bases of my thumbs were bruised from the crutches and I was pretty fed up. But at least on the boat I was getting a change of scenery.

Two days later we reached Lower Lough Erne. We paused in Kesh, a town with a jig named for it, accessed via the narrow Kesh River. At the entrance to the river we took photos of two 'road' signs with a red diagonal line through a picture of a jet ski, signs that gave us pleasure, for although we were trying to embrace the various water sports on the river, jet skis remained baddies. Noise, wash, intense showing off and no skill.

From Kesh we went to Muckross, a bleak spot tucked round the corner from Kesh, made bleaker by poor weather. There were good walks from here so Joe went off with the dogs, leaving me to brood in the boat. There were a lot of sports boats here too, but fortunately it was Tuesday and raining. Joe returned with reports from other walkers about the number of water-skiers and wake boarders who went out from Muckross. *Winter Solstice* rocked gently, pulling at her elasticated lines.

We didn't go to Belleek this time but we did travel the length of the broad lough, taking the right-hand route down the northern shore past Lusty Beg, a place highly recommended but out-of-bounds to us with our dogs. At the end of the lake we found Castle Caldwell, a heavily forested area with little to offer but fishing, a few walks (no good for me) and, we learned, a venue for sports boats coming from Muckross. Time to leave.

Chapter Twelve

'Ropes loosened river very high,' said the text. It was from Charlie Mackey in Athy. On 4 June 2007 we'd set out from Shannon Harbour to spend another summer on the River Barrow. The trip to Athy was uneventful, and we left *Winter Solstice* outside Charlie's house at Ardreigh Lock for a couple of weeks. In July it began to rain. And rained some more. Not the soft drizzle of a typical Irish summer but monsoon drops that swelled the rivers until they burst their banks. We'd thought little of it until Charlie's text.

As we were driving to the boat my mobile rang. It was Jean, our friend from Dublin, checking arrangements for the following day, when she would be joining us.

'Will we be cruising down Athy Main Street?' she asked. I laughed and made some class of a joke. It was only when we pulled up at Ardreigh that we understood what she meant. The canal had risen so much we had to mountaineer up the boarding-plank. We walked the hundred metres or so to the lock and watched the river torrenting by.

'It's no worse than the Shannon,' I said, but there was doubt in my voice.

Mid-morning Saturday and Jean arrived. Joe and I were thinking about bridges. The Barrow is spanned by beautiful but low arches. Would we be able to get under? Jean and I drove our two vehicles the couple of miles downriver to Maganey Bridge and had a look.

'Should be OK,' I said, reluctant to abandon our plans, especially as Jean was here ready for a cruise. The river was a bit fast, but we'd fit under no problem. We left Jean's car at the bridge – no point in being over-confident and taking it further downstream. Back to the boat and we cast off from our mooring, motoring to the lock. I dropped Joe and nudged *Winter Solstice* into the chamber. Joe did his business with racks and sluices, opened the lower gates and we cruised into the river. I picked Joe up in the relative calm below the lock (where a new jetty had been installed) and turned into the stream. This was nothing like the slowly flow-ing waters we'd known in 2005. Already we were gathering pace. On a river you have to travel faster than the current, otherwise you lose steerage. There was no prospect of slowing down.

We reached Maganey in just over an hour – record time – and I felt the first flutter of panic. A long island splits the river just before Maganey Bridge, narrow-ing the navigation channel and increasing the flow of water. We had to pass through the middle arch and were approaching at an alarming rate. I began to doubt my earlier judgement, seeing our timber boat smashed against stone pillars, but it was too late to do anything about it. I gripped the wheel and watched the island, then the bridge, then the island. As the slice of land finished I wrenched the wheel to the right, we jinked then straightened up as the river bore us towards the waiting arch. It looked so very, very low.

We roared through, foolishly ducking our heads, and shot out the other side. I did a handbrake turn onto the jetty. I was shaking as we tied up.

'Jesus,' I said. 'I need a drink.'

The dogs were delighted to be let out so soon after setting off and sniffed about as we watched the ridiculous flow on the Barrow. This was July for God's sake. We went for a walk along the towpath, had cups of tea and cake, then Jean and I went back to Ardreigh for our car. We had resigned ourselves to going no further that day. Before Jean left, a big, black Jeep turned through the gate of the small car park beside the bridge and onto the towpath. The driver stopped and introduced herself as Rita. She agreed it was mad and suggested we come down to the lock. She lived in the lock cottage and assured us it was very nice down there. We could bring our car down if we needed to.

After Jean left, Joe and I walked the kilometre or so to the lock with the dogs. It *was* a nice spot. We moved the boat, deciding to wait for the water to go down. Rita invited us in for tea. Later, when the lock-keeper paused for a chat, he laughed at our idea of going downstream.

'You'll never get under Carlow Bridge,' he said. 'Not with the river like this.'

We spent the next two days at the lock, where we received great hospitality from Rita and Edel in the lock cottage. Sunshine, rain, sunshine. Joe decided this would be a good time to replace one of the windows. After all, we weren't going anywhere. I gave him a look.

'It won't take long,' he said. 'All I have to do is …'

Half an hour later the window was out, a thunderstorm was raging and I was on the bank with a golf umbrella while Joe cursed and got silicone sealant all over the glass and his hands and the deck. The dogs shivered in the dog house.

Eventually the storm passed and the sun came out. Joe glued the window back in. I placed sticks at various points on the partially flooded lower jetty to mark the levels, checking them at regular intervals. The water went down. The lock-keeper appeared and told us there was still no possibility of getting under Carlow Bridge.

'But look,' I said, gesturing at my sticks. 'It's going down.'

'Not for long,' said the lock-keeper. Over the following couple of hours the marker sticks disappeared once more. We moved *Winter Solstice* to above the lock where she was under the watchful eye of our new friends and went home.

★★★

We never did get any further down the Barrow that summer. Floods were reported from around the country, and rivers were almost at winter levels. Finally, towards the end of August, there was a promise of better weather and we returned to Maganey to bring *Winter Solstice* home along the Grand Canal. By the time we reached Tullamore it was hot and sunny. We knew the Fleadh Ceol na hÉireann was just beginning its first year in the town and thought we'd stop off to see if anyone we knew was there. Tullamore has a pleasing little harbour, but it's bordered by a road so not good for dog walking. We stopped instead just before it and hammered stakes into the bank, walked into the centre and bought supplies, then put on shorts and sat on deck playing tunes. Maybe we'd stay the night.

That evening we headed into town with flute and banjo to find the pubs full of jigs and reels. Musicians stood in doorways and sat on window-ledges playing tunes from Roscommon and Sligo and Clare. There were a few exotics from England and Holland and America. Alongside all this were classes, mostly attended by children, and the all-Ireland competitions, a culmination of months of local, then county, then provincial competitions in every traditional instrument and in voice. The Fleadh is the Big Event for Comhaltas Ceoltóiri Éireann, the organisation that promotes traditional Irish music and culture around the world, and whatever you might think about the business of endless competitions for children, the buzz at the Fleadh was tremendous.

And we had the weather. Finally. A couple of other boats pulled in behind us. The dogs lay on the bank or on the side deck in the sunshine. Musician friends from Clare arrived, and we found a couple of pubs we liked to play tunes in. One of them, we were told, was the drinking hole of then Minister for Finance Brian Cowen. Sure enough he turned up one night and had a couple of pints, then sang a song. Fine voice. He looked better in real life than in photos.

A late night. I was asleep then I was awake. Someone had stepped on board. I kept very still, listening. Nothing. No dogs barking. Surely they would. The boat rocked slightly, then a splash. I jumped out of bed and was through the saloon in a few strides, telling the surprised and sleepy dogs to stay. It was very early but it was light. Standing on the aft deck I could see the cause of the disturbance floundering in the middle of the canal. He was little more than a teenager.

'What are you doing?' I said indignantly. How dare he use my boat as a spring board. He mumbled and thrashed.

'What are you doing?' I said, louder this time. He began to sink. I stared at him in disbelief then scrambled along the side deck to the life ring.

'Grab this,' I said, and threw it. He moved clumsily, slowly towards it. He was completely scuttered. So drunk he couldn't speak. I kept talking and he got hold of the ring. I pulled him in.

'I'm bringing you round the back of the boat,' I said. 'Hold tight.'

'Nmmggvvrull,' he said, but he hung on. Then I had to persuade him up the ladder, one slow rung at a time.

Eventually he stood dripping onto the after deck. I was eager to get him off the boat and encouraged him towards the shore, but he was determined to empty his boots first in that obstinate way drunks have. We did it together then I held his hand as he stumbled across the plank, praying he wouldn't tumble into the gap between bank and boat. He staggered about on the grass, saying he was going to his friends. At least he could talk again. I watched him anxiously, but it was light, the weather was warm and he was heading away from the water.

Joe was still asleep! I woke him up.

'I just pulled someone out of the water,' I said. I needed a witness to the fact I hadn't dreamt it. Joe looked at me woozily and turned over. He obviously thought that I'd been dreaming.

Next morning I saw the overgrown boy with his mates. I recognised the boots.

'Are your boots wet?' I asked him.

'Yes.' He laughed, looked bewildered.

'Do you remember me pulling you out of the canal early this morning?'

'No! You didn't!'

'That's how your boots got wet. You went up my boarding-plank and fell in. You were sinking.' He looked as though it was the funniest story he'd ever heard.

After the Fleadh we took *Winter Solstice* along the canal to Shannon Harbour and left her there. That was the end of boating for the year. We'd lost heart, somehow, with all the terrible weather, but also Joe had managed to wangle a spot in the big shed, a massive structure with a corrugated roof, open at the sides and full of pigeons. Over the winter he spent several weekends removing the 1960s aluminium windows, secure in the knowledge that even in a thunderstorm she would remain dry, then, with the help of friend Dominic, he replaced them with timber. At the same time he stained the coach-house sides in a final attempt to make the wood look decent, and behold! A boat transformed! One which, I sincerely hoped, would be waterproof. I was tired of waking in the night to the drip on my pillow. In the end we painted the decks too – it was easier than washing off the pigeon shit.

★★★

In 2008, we waited for summer to begin. It was wet and windy and cold enough to need a fire. We had a couple of big projects going on at home – a new conservatory to protect us from rain and midges, and some major garden work. Joe talked of selling *Winter Solstice*. What was the point of a boat when we weren't using it? I resisted. How could we possibly abandon our beloved? You didn't have to be always using something to justify having it. You could have a year off. And we had the dinghy. We should learn to use that properly.

The dinghy was a 1958 Yachting World Day Boat, made from beautiful timber but in need of care, given to us in the hope that we might keep it going. We had recently completed a sailing course at the University of Limerick Activity Centre on Lough Derg. The one-person training dinghies were bright yellow and extremely unstable. We spent a considerable amount of time being tipped into the water – I don't think I've ever been so cold in all my life in spite of the wetsuits – but we loved it and wanted to do more.

The Yachting World Day Boat was heavy, a steady cruising dinghy, unlikely to tip over, with the name *Swallow* in faded paint on the transom. It was a while since she'd been in the water. There was leakage around the centre-board casing. The first time we put her in the water at Ducey's Pier at the sheltered, Scarriff end of Lough Derg, she 'took up' so much water she immediately sank two feet to the bottom. We lifted her, brought her home, dried her out and Joe did some emergency work. On the second launch she stayed afloat. We hadn't intended to do more than launch her, see if she floated, and take her home again. But what harm? We put up the jib, the small sail at the bow, just to try it out. The wind at our back filled the sail and we drifted silently through tall reeds. Our maiden voyage! We grinned at each other.

'It's so quiet,' I said. A dabchick trilled, giving the silence emphasis. We didn't intend to sail into the bay as we had no mainsail up. Nor did we have a mainsheet, having left home without the new rope bought for this purpose: we had raised the jib simply as an experiment. *Swallow*, although afloat, still leaked badly, requiring frequent attention from the bilge pump. We were carried away, however, by the silent joy of wind power.

Suddenly free of the reeds we went back and forth a few times, delighted with ourselves. A cruiser pulled out from a hidden gap in the shore and we managed to turn away from it. We barely noticed the creeping of the boat to the east and away from the harbour where we'd launched. It was only as the wind freshened we thought we should head for home, but a boat will not sail head to wind, and one cannot tack without a mainsail.

By the time we took out the oars to row and drew down the jib, ripples had turned into small waves, and the land was slipping past the wrong way.

'I can't do it,' cried Joe. 'It's too much.' I watched as a small island surrounded by rocks drew closer. The sky threatened rain.

'Jesus. We'll have to land,' I said. How could we do it without damaging the boat or ourselves?

'Use the oars,' shouted Joe, struggling to bring them inside the boat. 'We need to slow down.' I grabbed hold of one and we began jabbing at the lakebed. There was a grinding sound, *Swallow* pivoted like a car at the Waltzers, then settled and was still. We sat in silence, briefly resisting the temptation to apportion blame.

'It was stupid going out without the mainsail,' said Joe. I didn't say it wasn't I who had suggested it.

'You left the mobile phone at home,' said Joe.

'I didn't think we'd actually go out,' I said accusingly.

We should, I suppose, have been thankful we were not further out in the bay where we could easily have been blown all the way to Tipperary. We waded ashore with the painter, attached it to a rock to secure the dinghy, then examined our options. There was little boat traffic at this end of the lake, so rescue seemed unlikely, but the island was very close to the main shore, and reeds marked a possible causeway. Perhaps we'd be able to wade across.

We climbed up the bank, stopping at the top to look for boats. There were none. We turned, despondent, and walked to the 'causeway', peering into the reeds. It was difficult to see how deep it was, but we thought it might be feasible to cross. We stepped gingerly into the water and immediately sank, the water already above our knees. We looked at each other and climbed out again. We would certainly be up to our chests in water, maybe up to our necks or ears.

'Perhaps that boat will come back,' I said, but without much hope. We ate chocolate and looked miserably across the wave-topped water. The sunshine had disappeared as the wind dragged clouds from the west and I was shivering. It was no longer the weather for skimpy shorts. A dot of white appeared in the far reaches of the bay and we watched it approach. It was a hire boat heading into the Scarriff River, of no use to us. Then another white dot, a private boat this time.

The cruiser turned, and without need to speak we leapt up and down, windmill-armed. I took off my bright yellow buoyancy aid and waved it in the air as Joe scrambled down the bank. The cruiser stopped then began to head towards us very slowly: this little bay was shallow except for the channel to the harbour. The boat stopped again, but this time within shouting distance.

'We're stuck,' yelled Joe. 'Can you tow us off?' The man looked sceptical.

'You'd have to get the dinghy into deeper water.'

'Yes, yes, we will!' Joe untied the painter and waded in, but three attempts to steer the boat through choppy water against the prevailing wind failed. I tried not to cry.

'Can you throw us a rope?' said Joe. Our rescuer did, but it dropped short. A second attempt and Joe caught it, fumbling with cold fingers as he tried to attach it to the front of the dinghy. Surely the cruiser crew would give up on us. Then it was tied on and we pushed while they pulled on the rope. We made some progress and decided to climb in, but it was still too shallow and the boat went aground. We tried again, pushing out further. Jumping into a high-sided dinghy when waist high in lake is not easy. In fact, if asked could I do such a thing, I would have said no, but it's astonishing what adrenalin and desperation will do to one's leaping skills. With a few scrapes and muttered swearings both Joe and I were aboard.

We felt very silly. Our rescuers towed us into a safe harbour, where we had to explain how we'd got into such a fix. We were economical with the truth, but our foolishness was undeniable. We left the dinghy where it was and dripped our way along the road to where we'd left the car. We learned more about dinghy sailing and our own folly during that afternoon on the lake than we ever would have done had things gone well.

Towards the end of summer, having had our fill of sailing *Swallow* on Lough Graney, our local lake, and with the weather a little more settled, we made a snap decision to return to the Fleadh, in Tullamore for a second year. In 2007 we'd had the company of a few boats along the bank of the main line and the harbour was busy enough, but word had got out. That year the Offaly branch of the IWAI had organised a 'Float to the Fleadh' to encourage those canal-shy Shannon skippers to taste the delights of the Grand. They were doing it again in 2008, and this time half the Shannon and Barrow was going.

Many of the boats had travelled ahead the weekend before the eight-day Fleadh and were tucked up safe, but some were due to leave Shannon Harbour on the weekend it began. We had no desire to queue for the locks, so gave them a couple of days' head start. We left Portumna on Monday afternoon, pulling into a swollen Shannon with levels more typical of January than August. The flow was strong and it took us longer than usual to make the trip to Shannon Harbour. In the lock that raises you from river to canal, Jason, the lock-keeper, gave us the news. The rump end of the Float to the Fleadh was stuck in Pollagh, halfway to Tullamore, because the canal was impassable beyond this point. Floods had caused havoc.

Water levels were down a little the following day, and the sun was shining, so we set out to see how far we could get. We reached Pollagh and the half-dozen boats still tied to the jetty waiting for the return of their skippers the following weekend. The canal was full but not overflowing so we carried on, eventually stopping for the night below Lock 31 at Cornalour. We let the dogs out and Aoife hopped onto the aft deck, barking ferociously at the water. We paused in our fussing with ropes to see what the trouble was. Great islands of froth were floating past on the flow from the lock. We'd never seen so much. It was as though we'd tied up in a bubble bath.

There was water lying in the fields alongside the canal. Acres and acres of it. We were puzzling over this when lock-keeper Alan Lindley appeared. He told us the canal had been in flood between Ballycommon (just above Tullamore) and Edenderry, and the banks had been in imminent danger of breaching. Not only would this cause terrible flooding and possible mud slides, it would be a major engineering repair job. Alan and other local lock-keepers had received emergency calls in the middle of the night and had leapt to their posts. The canal was closed temporarily while they tried to deal with the volume of water.

First they opened the racks on every lock gate and left them open all weekend in hope of relieving pressure on the canal banks. It didn't work. In a final attempt to prevent the threatened breach, they opened the emergency sluices below Lock 31, releasing excess water into the adjoining fields. The land was designated for this purpose, but the cattle in those fields didn't know that. There was some loss of livestock. It was fifty years since the sluices had been opened like this, and there hadn't been such rainfall and flooding within living memory.

Up into the lock at 10.30 next morning and brown foam filled the chamber as the rush of peaty water brought us up to the next level. This soft water that runs off the bogs has a soapiness about it that froths whenever the water is agitated. Our small river at home does the same, setting up white-topped whirlpools that look like pirouetting whipped-cream gateaux. A neighbour told me that if you've been working on the bog stacking turf the best way to clean your peat-browned hands is to wash them in peaty water.

Alan told us the canal was clear to Tullamore. We kept going, arriving at 1 p.m., *Winter Solstice* looking filthy with her brown-stained hull. At the jetty beside the Tullamore Dew Heritage Centre we paused to scrub her clean before heading for the same bank we'd inhabited the previous year. But our bank was filled with other boats. How dare they? We would either have to go way down the line or, hang on a minute, couldn't we sneak in here at the corner? Most of the boats already there were HBA barges with a bigger draught than us. We banged in our stakes and pulled *Winter Solstice* as close to the bank as possible, bridging the gap with our plank.

In Tullamore we discovered the extent of the flooding around the country. Not only had there been record levels of rainfall, but people had been driven out of houses recently built on flood plains. Carlow had suffered badly – apartments built on Centaur Street beside the Barrow, a river with a history of regular flooding, suffered particularly badly, with over a hundred people evacuated by the Civil Defence. Drainage systems were overwhelmed by water, raw sewage was washed into streets and houses. All those

clever developers making millions seemed to have forgotten – or didn't care – that floodwater had to go
somewhere.

The rain mostly kept away. We stayed four nights in
Tullamore then returned to Shannon Harbour, doing
the trip in one go. We put *Winter Solstice* to bed for the
winter and went home.

Chapter Thirteen

*B*y 2009, we were more than ready for a good boating season. There was no more talk of selling *Winter Solstice* and she was looking smarter than she had for a while – Joe spent a week in Scarriff Harbour, where we kept her over the winter, leaning down from the harbour wall or flailing about in our small inflatable dinghy while he painted the topsides of the hull. The forecast for early summer was good, and we decided to take our holidays at the beginning of June. A new year, and we'd pushed aside memories of a rain-sodden, flooded countryside.

The June bank holiday, a heatwave on Lough Derg, and we joined an IWAI Cruise-in-Company, something we hadn't done in years. We had a new (second-hand) dinghy, secure from leaks as the hull was (whisper it) fibreglass. We hadn't gone completely the plastic route, however: she was a cruising dinghy similar to *Swallow* with *lots* of timber. Unlike *Swallow* she was gaff rigged, with mast and sails that were easy to raise and lower, and that would fit inside the boat when she was on the trailer. Another plus was that it didn't take an hour of swearing to launch and unlaunch her as the trailer was well designed. She didn't come with a name, so sometimes we called her *An Báidín Gorm*, the small blue boat, but mostly she was just the dinghy.

The Cruise-in-Company began in Mountshannon with a trip to Castlebawn, a restored tower house in Scarriff Bay known locally as Simon's Castle. We'd passed this tower many times when cruising to and from the Scarriff River, and seen it when driving the road to Killaloe, but never had the chance to visit. It was built by the McNamara clan around 1540, but was confiscated in the 1650s when Cromwell was busy planting Parliamentarian soldiers in Ireland. It became derelict but remained intact until 1827, difficult to get to by land or water so used on and off as a handy place to distil poitín. Eventually the authorities had enough of playing cat and mouse with the distillers and took the explosives route. The tower was tough and hung on to three of its walls until, in 1996, Pat and Mary Cody bought the place and set about restoring it. In 2009 it was open to the public during July and August or by appointment.

The only access to Castlebawn was by boat – for the Codys as well as visitors – and there were good though limited jetties. We had to rationalise boats, so brought the Goggins with us on *Winter Solstice*. The Codys had done an astonishing job, creating a comfortable home, but always with a sense of the building's history. We climbed to the top of the tower to gain a very different perspective of Scarriff Bay.

On Sunday we moved on. As we pulled out of Mountshannon I slowed *Winter Solstice* to a crawl while Joe pulled the dinghy alongside and made her fast, bow and stern, to the deck cleats, a couple of fenders between to keep both vessels safe. It took longer than expected. Every type of watercraft within miles seemed to be on the lake – each time Joe had her almost attached, a boat would rip past creating wash and he had to abort the manoeuvre, but eventually we were doubled up and I put on a bit of speed. There was a terrible crashing noise. I slowed and Joe adjusted the ropes. More crashing.

'Maybe we could pull her behind us,' I said cautiously.

'Mmm,' said Joe doubtfully, but a few minutes later he detached the dinghy and let her travel to the back as I eased forward. Ten minutes later he had two lines leading from the front of the dinghy to the posts on the aft deck of *Winter Solstice*. I picked up speed. It seemed OK, so I opened the throttle some more.

'Slow down!'

'OK, OK. No need to shout.' More adjustments and off we went again. The dinghy seemed more settled this time. *Winter Solstice* didn't complain.

We travelled north, halfway up the lake to Rossmore, wearing shorts and sunglasses. Long pink tongues hung limp from the dogs' mouths. The lake was flat and reflected the blue of the sky. The contrast with the previous two years couldn't be greater. No use for sailing though. We kept an eye on the many flags drooping from masts in the hope of a breeze but there was none until, late on Sunday afternoon, we saw a couple of ripples on the water. Not exactly the cat's paws that would indicate proper wind, but a start. We hopped into the dinghy, started the outboard and motored into the open lake. Up with the sail and away we didn't go. We'd have to wait for another day.

At the end of the holiday weekend we continued upriver, leaving the dinghy behind on its trailer. The heatwave continued. At Meelick, lads were leaping into the water below the lock. I swam more sedately in the canal above. Upstream to Banagher, then past the entrance to Shannon Harbour and the Grand Canal. The old Shannonbridge chimney appeared in the distance, its red stripes teasing with a 'Nearly there' call, drifting away as we turned another bend in the river, teasing again as we came close. We idly commented on this original, now decommissioned, chimney, the new one sitting pale and uninteresting beside it. Will they leave it there, we wondered. It would be a shame to see it go.

Later that month, on 25 June, we read in *The Irish Times* that the chimney had been demolished. Derry Killeen, who had worked at the plant for over forty years, was quoted as wondering how people on the river would navigate without its guiding presence. We wondered the same.

After Shannonbridge, Athlone, and ideas of spending some time on Lough Ree, a lake which, along with many other people, we'd only crossed in order to go elsewhere. In Athlone Joe dug out his tin of paint to continue the job he'd started in Scarriff

– topsides done, he wanted to smarten up the coach-house roof. There was one big black cloud in the sky, so I suggested he might hold off for a while, but he was having none of it. The job would be done. We were tied to the old wall on the Roscommon side of the river from where you can stroll through the water meadows below Athlone Lock so I took the dogs for a walk. I brought my umbrella. The reeds were as tall as me with narrow pathways between. Aoife roared up and down these 'tunnels', while Frankie ran on ahead. A few fat drops of rain rustled through the reeds. The black cloud released its load. By the time I got back to the boat the dogs were soaked, as was my umbrella, and another, smaller black cloud sat over *Winter Solstice*.

Next morning Joe had to wash long dribbles of paint off the windows before we could set out for Lough Ree. It was sunny again and, more important, windless. Part way up the lake we turned east, bisecting it to reach the Inny, a twisty, sweet little river that we'd heard had a bank suitable for mooring. We chugged along as far as the bridge at the end of the Navigation, turned *Winter Solstice* and went halfway back before stopping for lunch, hammering in pegs and putting out the boarding-plank. After sandwiches, Joe returned to the paint job rudely interrupted in Athlone while I sat on a folding chair in a cow-patted field with the dogs and played my flute. I got through, I think, one set of reels before a shadow settled over our pastoral scene. I looked behind to see dark clouds and sniffed the air – definitely a whiff of rain. In front, the lake still glittered.

We made a decision. Joe went into overdrive on the painting, while I pulled out the stakes, got dogs, self and boarding-plank onto the boat and started the engines. Two drops of rain on the windscreen. I set off downriver. On the lake the sun was still shining, and we went south along the eastern shore, keeping an eye on the clouds, passing a boat cruising slowly north. We did the usual wave of acknowledgement. Three drops of rain. 'Turn round!' cried Joe. 'It's brighter back there. There's a big cloud ahead.' I put on the brakes and turned while Joe went into triple drive with the paintbrush. We passed the boat that had passed us and we saluted each other again. Four drops of rain. 'Go back! The cloud's up here now.' I turned once more, passing the northbound boat. Puzzled faces at the window. This time we kept going, the clouds having moved on to torment someone else. By the time we reached Killinure Point at the south of the lake, the coach-house roof was done.

★★★

We turned off the Shannon into the Boyle River, approaching Cootehall once more, the sailing dinghy bobbing along behind *Winter Solstice*. It was July, we'd launched our small boat at Drumsna and were on our way to Lough Key for some sailing. Drawing into the village, we came alongside the quay wall just below the bridge. From here the river looked much the same as it had in 2006 – the banks were high so our surroundings were hidden. Walking up to the road, however, things couldn't have been more different. The billboard advertising Oakport, the new housing estate, was still there, the estate Brian McDonald of the *Independent* had enthused about on 23 October 2006, writing 'Deal includes river cruiser and golf membership – for less than €300,000. NO DOUBT about it, it's the property deal of the year.' The billboard had faded, along with hopes of prosperity.

Writer John McGahern would hardly recognise the village. He lived in the Barracks here when his father was sergeant, describing the Cootehall of that time as being:

> ...scattered randomly about a big triangular field, Henry's field. No two shops or houses adjoined one another, and they were set down as haphazardly as if they had been carried there on various breezes. There was a church, a post office, the barracks, a presbytery, two shops, three bars, a few houses.

There's a plaque in McGahern's memory overlooking the lake beside the Barracks. In July 2009, the village was still scattered about, but forty-six new houses had taken over the big triangular field: thirty three-bedroom semi-detached, five bungalows and one detached. Only three were occupied, two as holiday homes by people from Dublin and one by a local family. On the road from the river three retail units were ready to service the needs of all the new people on the estate. They were as the builders left them.

The estate had a desolate, unfinished look about it. On a rise at the top end of the village was another estate of bigger, detached houses. Some were occupied but many of the newest were not. People talked about what would happen to these houses if nobody ever lived in them – Ireland's climate is deleterious to empty properties. In 2007, Alice Lyons captured the mood of the place on Cute Hall, a website of writing from Cootehall:

> As I write this, the thundering booms from the diggers resound all around me. In Cootehall, 100 plus new homes are being constructed. All in the name of rural renewal, but for that you should read "whopping tax break". The village could have done with a bit more life. A few more dwellings and shops. But, oy vey. You wouldn't recognize it. The spring weather brought all the Cootehall denizens out of hibernation. And we just stood around on the road and gave out about all the building and our dirty windows and about how we should have done something about it before it was too late. Well, it's too late.

I returned from my walk to find Joe in conversation with Brendan Corrigan, who lived on a boat in Cootehall Marina across the bridge, come over to admire *Winter Solstice*. He was one of those who'd bought a house on the new estate. Things had not turned out as expected, he said, and he was rather regretting his decision to buy. As was the Dublin man whose purchase of an

Oakport semi-detached had not delivered the promised lifestyle. Living in a ghost estate was not what he had in mind, and he was upset at the lack of a private marina. He was expecting a berth. None was forthcoming. The advertising in 2009, to be fair, did not say there would be a berth. Only that, along with your free boat, you would get use of a private slipway in a private marina. Not the same thing at all. I wonder how many non-boating people would know that.

Many houses on the estate were for sale, though the same house varied in price from €160,000 to €265,000 depending on which auctioneer you consulted. The free boat was no longer mentioned, but there was still a proposed private helipad (subject to planning). What were people thinking? This was a very ordinary estate of houses. Were Mam or Dad going to go to work in nearby Carrick by chopper? Or was this for the people flying down from Dublin for weekends in their second home?

In 2006, Ireland was a country giddy with its own notions of success. Developers thought little of paying €3,500 an hour to Celtic Helicopters, Ireland's best-known helicopter charter company, to save them a journey by car or train. Properties were sold before they were built as expectations of profit became the norm. Shane Tully, the developer of the Oakport site, said in the 2006 *Independent* interview:

> We build about 100 houses a year and last year we built a development in Tubbercurry and

gave away a new Opel Corsa to anyone who bought a house. We are now looking at another development in a fishing area, but you'll have to watch this space for what we are going to offer in that one.

There was a collective madness whose echoes were evident in 2009. There was still absurd advertising for lifestyles people could no longer afford. The blurb on the Quay West website, another Roscommon development with private marina, trilled :

> Imagine rising on Saturday morning in Quay West, get the family and friends organised and perhaps have breakfast in Bruno's before you start up your Drago cruiser in Port Alainn marina ... no journey planned! ... so where to, you ask? ... well how about cruising up to Enniskillen (take in some shopping too!) and soon the Ulster Canal will be opening so its [*sic*] Belfast "here we come" ...

This may cause a few difficulties for the unwary skipper. To reach Enniskillen you have to navigate the Ballinamore-Ballyconnell canal, the first section of the Shannon-Erne Waterway, with its thirty-one locks, average cruising time eighteen hours. Then you would have to put wheels on your boat to travel along the non-existent Ulster Canal, which would take some years to be rebuilt. And finally, perhaps, a set of wings to fly you to Belfast as the canal, should it ever be redeveloped, will end at Lough Neagh nearly 20 miles north-west of Belfast.

After three days' sailing on Lough Key and walking round the wooded grounds of the Forest Park we rejoined the Shannon, travelling north along the narrowing river. Approaching Leitrim Village we came to a fork in the waterway, let the Shannon Navigation continue on its way to Lough Allen and kept right for the village and Shannon-Erne Waterway. In early 2009 Captain Joe Gillespie of Waterways Ireland (WI) had told me that ownership of the new Leitrim jetties would shortly be transferred from the developer to WI, so we were expecting them to be attached to the land. Indeed, work was in progress on the WI end of the bridge that gave access to car park and toilet block. 'We won't be joining them up yet,' said the workman beside the temporary tape barrier. They were still waiting for the developer to sort out his side of the land bridge. WI couldn't take over responsibility until this was done as there'd be no safe access to the facilities in the harbour. Stalemate.

To reach the road from the new jetties you had to cross a broad and clearly temporary plank, then pick your way through a muddy gap between wall and construction fence. Each summer since the jetties were put in someone had taken down the red-and-white tape blocking access from the water and laid a plank to the land. There was nothing WI could do about it as the jetties were on private property.

That evening we took a walk through the village. Apartments and a hotel crowded the water's edge and the outskirts were overwhelmed by new houses. A few of the apartments were in use as holiday homes but many of the houses on the estates stood empty. Later, in The Barge, a steak-house and pub at the top of the main street, I talked to proprietors John and Rose Pierce. From their point of view all this building hadn't done the place any good. According to John there were at least 170 apartments and houses empty, and his business hadn't improved. I was told of how all those ducks who'd made the old river bank so mucky had been driven out from loss of habitat or, according to the more suspicious locals, eaten by Polish and German construction workers.

The building boom had left a legacy of unfinished and unwanted buildings on some of the most beautiful reaches of the river. Leitrim, Longford and parts of Roscommon had been designated tax incentive areas, supposedly to attract investment but in reality giving tax breaks to people who didn't need them. Tax relief was allowed for expenditure incurred in building or buying a property that would be let to tenants, but there seemed to be no thought at all about who was actually going to live in these houses in a part of the country where there was limited work.

Planning permission was granted for riverside sites on the north Shannon and its main tributary, the Boyle. All the small villages were sprouting identikit houses in rows or crescents. The waterway was becoming littered with unwanted properties that would, before long, become damp and dreary. Short-term gain instead of long-term well-being. While construction

was going on all over the country it was (just) possible to convince ourselves the money would continue
to flow. Certainly the exchequer benefited from the
taxes, but now all the houses were complete, the Poles
and Latvians had gone home and the glut of identical,
ill-conceived housing estates was all that was left to
remind us of the good times.

There are a few villages that have not been despoiled,
reminding us of what has been lost. Drumsna is one
of these, a Leitrim village on a big lazy bend of the
Shannon. The landlady of McLoughlin's bar told me
how a few years ago a fellow came in looking for the
owner of the field down by the harbour. Is that field
yours? he asked the landlady. It was.

'I'll sign a cheque for you now. Half a million.'

The landlady told him she had no interest and to
take himself away. The place was more important to
her than money. Five other landowners did the same.
The result is an area with pride of place and a display
of local history that seems to be missing from those
other disfigured villages. There are no empty riverside
apartments or ranks of identical houses.

There were, it seemed to us, fewer boats on the water,
even during the fine weather of 2009's summer. In the
marinas 'For Sale' signs were being pasted to the windows of expensive cruisers. I felt we'd been taken back
eight years to the days when smaller, older Freemans
and Brooms were the norm. Those of us on the river
who enjoyed the camaraderie of a gentler, more cour-
teous time will not be unhappy with the returning

calm. Neither will the wildlife disrupted by boats that travelled too fast, their skippers apparently having no concern for anyone but themselves. The disarray caused by overstretched bank accounts, lost jobs and ruinous overbuilding will blight Irish lives for many years to come.

In September we brought *Winter Solstice* back to Shannon Harbour, where we put her into the dry dock. The hull was painted and anti-fouled, then surveyed by John Lefroy to make sure her planks were sound. She was, he said, in excellent condition. Would probably outlast the two of us. A sobering thought.

Epilogue

*I*n the evening light I stood in Cootehall looking through trees at Oakport Lake. Before me, on a lectern, was a plaque bearing John McGahern's words:

> **A white moon rested on the water.**
> **There was no wind.**
> **The stars in their places were clear and fixed.**
> **Who would want change since change will come**
> **without wanting?**
> **Who this night would not want to live?**

Later we sat in the cockpit below the bridge against the quay wall. Mist drifted, riding on the current. Two swans made white pillows as they slept on the water, their cygnets between them. They too were drifting with the current, but less quickly than the mist – they were propelling gently in their sleep. As I watched, each parent in turn unwound its neck from slumber, shivered down its length and looked about. A porcelain sculpture floating in dry ice. All was well. The babies slept on. Change may come but nothing changes.

When we first began boating, in the days of *Caoimhe,* a friend told us how he envied our fledgling status on the river. There is a wonder in exploring the new that can never be recaptured. However, there is also great joy in the return, reacquainting oneself with the forgotten, meeting new people. In 2009, Joe, the dogs and I spent weeks on the river and I fell in love with *Winter Solstice* and the Shannon all over again. I am no longer anxious about turning sideways in a lock or going aground, not because these things will never happen but because I know from experience how to deal with them.

In spite of changes in villages along the way, the majority of the waterway is unspoiled. We are astonishingly fortunate in Ireland to have rivers and canals with public harbours that anyone can use with few of the prohibitive expenses found in many other European countries that make boating a pastime only for the wealthy. There is still nothing like setting out on a clear morning to meander along the river, or sitting in the cockpit with a glass of chilled wine as the sun goes down over the lake.

Who, any night on the river, would not want to live?

Acknowledgments

*T*hank you to fellow boaters Brian Goggin and Tom Bailey for various nuggets of information, and to the many members of the IWAI who have given their help and advice along the way.

Thanks also to Adrian Frazier, for title suggestions and setting this book in motion, and to editor Eoin Purcell for taking it the rest of the way.

Finally, thanks to the mate of this story, my husband Joe, for his companionship, support and encouragement.